Moogavani Pillanagrovi

D1715675

OXFORD NOVELLAS
Encompassing literature, popular and genre fiction,
writers old and new, this series presents an orchestra
of Indic voices

Series Editor: Mini Krishnan

Other titles in the Series

Vaadivaasal (Tamil)
   C.S. Chellappa

Tyanantar (Marathi)
   Saniya

Sheet Sahasik Hemantolok (Bengali)
   Nabaneeta Dev Sen

Dweepa (Kannada)
   Na. D'Souza

*Jeevichirikkunnavarkku
Vendiyulla Oppees* (Malayalam)
   Johny Miranda

Moogavani Pillanagrovi
Ballad of Ontillu

Kesava Reddy

Translated from Telugu by the Author

Revised by
J.K. Snyder

OXFORD
UNIVERSITY PRESS

OXFORD
UNIVERSITY PRESS

Oxford University Press is a department of the University of Oxford.
It furthers the University's objective of excellence in research, scholarship,
and education by publishing worldwide. Oxford is a registered trademark of
Oxford University Press in the UK and in certain other countries

Published in India by
Oxford University Press
YMCA Library Building, 1 Jai Singh Road, New Delhi 110 001, India

ISBN-13: 978-0-19-809742-6
ISBN-10: 0-19-809742-5

Typeset in Berling LT Std 10/15.5,
at MAP Systems, Bengaluru 560 082, India
Printed in India at Akash Press, New Delhi 110 020

CONTENTS

CONTENTS

Series Editor's Note

*'Freedom is knowing and understanding things
quite other than ourselves.'*

–Anonymous

Writers have always experimented with forms in their search
for the best vehicles for their thoughts, moods, and words.
While there might be arguments about what length defines
the genre, the novella was shaped and recognized in the late
nineteenth century as allowing for greater development
of theme and character than a short story without being
burdened with the demands of a full-length novel.

Our broad goal in assembling the Oxford Novellas,
a unique series combining substance and brevity, is to
present the least studied genre from one of the world's
oldest literary traditions which includes one of the
most sophisticated pre-modern poetic theories. At a

time when news is entertainment and literature has to compete with popular fiction, two criteria have guided our selections: socially relevant themes for readers who might want to know things quite outside their experience and understanding, and literary excellence. Thus, famous names march with writers few people have even heard of.

Having absorbed words from nearly four hundred languages, English is opulently equipped to interpret and express the cultural energy of the regions it once entered as the colonizer's voice. If, to paraphrase Wittgenstein, the limits of our language mark the limits of our world, we hope, from time to time, through this series, to move the borders of literary enjoyment further and ever further. Translation into English brings together the creative potential of different Indian languages, the special understanding of the world each one of those languages has, and consequently, the distinctive way they carry the memories and histories of those who use them.

The art of story-telling and the art of narration mingle to give us a literary mosaic made possible by translators working to move texts originally written in other languages into English. We believe that the translator is not merely an echo or a shadow, a reflection or a crib, but a fresh, strong supporting voice that conveys both the said and the equally vital 'unsaid' parts of the original into the receiving language.

MINI KRISHNAN

Author's Note

Moogavani Pillanagrovi is the story of Bakkireddy, a small farmer who met an unnatural end, and of his five acres of land which evolved into a *sthala-purana* (place-legend). When the book was first published in Telugu in 1993, a reader made a quick guess at my connection with the protagonist of the story and wrote me a letter addressing me as the grandson of Bakkireddy! It was a good guess, though slightly off the mark. I am not Bakkireddy's grandson, but his son. The reader's misjudgement was probably because the story was set far back in 1950. In fact, Bakkireddy died in 1964, and I wrote the story twenty-nine years later.

The thing that struck me most was my father's organic relationship with the land and the great innocence in which he lived and died. The relationship was so umbilical and primitive that he believed his land was endowed with vital, mental, and even spiritual elements, and was an organic being with a life of its own. He toiled on it ceaselessly till the last moment of his life. For all his devotion to the land, he never expected or obtained anything more than the minimum required for his subsistence. He really laboured out of a sense of duty as a farmer and for the love of his land.

This dispassionate action, *nishkamakarma*, of Bakkireddy must not be confused with the one espoused by the Bhagavad Gita; for the Gita exhorts man to dissociate himself from the results of action consciously, voluntarily, and actively. But Bakkireddy was not even aware of his rights and privileges to demand the fruits of his labour. For him, the socio-political and economic forces were as mysterious as the natural ones that caused calamities. Insofar as the forces were beyond his comprehension, he was conditioned to think that deprivation and suffering were to be endured silently and unquestioningly. That was how his father and fore-fathers had lived.

It is to celebrate this holy innocence that I wrote the story. But the celebration will not be meaningful unless the injustice meted out to the unfortunate man was redressed. However, as no redressment was possible on account of the plot which was rigid and inclement, I invoked the intervention of the Five Elements. The Five Elements came along and played their roles in a most graceful manner rendering poetic justice to the much-wronged man. And the people of the village, on their part, earnestly, reverently accepted and remembered the verdict of the Five Elements and they witnessed in their own lifetime, Bakkireddy's five acres turning into a sthala-purana.

* * *

I feel a little explanation is needed for the three minor characters in the story: the Village Administrator, the Village Accountant, and the Village Servant. The three posts are held traditionally and paid for by the State Government. The Village Administrator is responsible for law and order in the village; he also collects land taxes from the farmers and remits them to the Tahasildar. The Village Accountant prepares and maintains the various documents pertaining to the landed property of the villagers; he also functions as land surveyor. The Village Servant assists the two aforementioned officials. These posts were abolished when N.T. Rama Rao came to power in 1984.

* * *

I take this opportunity to express my heartfelt thanks to J.K. Snyder for his excellent help in translating the work into English language. My thanks are also due to Chidambaram Radha Krishna and Lux Jothi Kumar without whose initiative and concern this publication would not have materialized. My special thanks are due to Mini Krishnan for her valuable guidance and editorial support.

KESAVA REDDY

Introduction

Regional and Linguistic Context

Telugu is a south-central Dravidian language, the origin of which can be traced to many centuries before the birth of Christ. Telugu speakers have spread into Karnataka and Tamil Nadu and integrated into the local population in a way no other language community has. According to the *Aitreya Brahmana*, a commentary of the *Rigveda* (circa 1700–1100 BC), they lived on the southern side of the Vindya Range along with Pundras, Pulidas, Sabaras, and Mootibas. They were originally called the Andhras and the term 'Telugu' came much later. The etymology of 'Telugu' is not known for certain as some researchers think that it is derived from 'Trilinga' as in 'Trilinga

Desa', the country on whose boundaries stand three mountains – Kaleswara, Srisaila, and Bheemeswara with lingas atop all three. But some others argue that Telugu means white and 'unga' means the plural and hence it means white people.

The first reference to an Andhra kingdom can be seen in Sanskrit epics. During the Kurukshethra war, they along with the Kalingas, another branch of the same group, supported the Kauravas and during the Rajasuya Yagna conducted by Yudhishtira after the Kurukshethra war, Sahadeva defeated many countries including Andhra. The *Jataka Tales* (200–250 BC) which mentions the Andhras at the time of the death of the great Maurya king, Ashoka, is the first historical record.

The Satavahana dynasty which reigned for nearly 450 years ruled the first great empire of Andhra followed by the Ikshwaku (AD 575–1022) and Vijayanagara (AD 1336–1800). Andhra, Karnataka, and Maharashtra observe the same New Year Day as it is based on the Salivahana Era called after the great Satavahana king, Salivahana.

Telugu is acclaimed as one of the four classical languages of India. It ranks third by the number of its native speakers in India and thirteenth in the Ethnologue List of most spoken languages worldwide. Telugu borrowed many grammatical features from

Sanskrit. It is naturally an official language of the state of Andhra Pradesh and spoken by significant minorities in states like Tamil Nadu, Karnataka, Maharashtra, Odisha, Chhattisgarh, and the union territory of Puducherry. In all, it is the mother tongue of about 200 million Indians.

Though Telugu words appear in the Prakrit anthology of poems, *Gathasapthasathi* (first century BC) by the Satavahana king, Hala, the earliest epigraphic record of Telugu language dates to the sixth century. But the Bhattiprolu (Guntur district) inscription of 400 BC contains Telugu words. The first inscription entirely in Telugu, discovered in Rayalaseema region of Andhra Pradesh, is dated AD 575 and it is attributed to the Renati Cholas.

It has become customary to consider Nannaya as the Adikavi (first poet) of Telugu literature who wrote a part of the Mahabharata (AD 1022). It is a product of the period in which literary language was distinct from the popular language and many phonetic changes took place in the language. The major part of Mahabharata was written by Thikkana, an extraordinary poet (thirteenth century), and the remaining part by Errapreggada (fourteenth century). With the rise of *prabhanda*s in the hands of great poets like Allsaani Peddana, Nandi Thimmana, Raamaraajabhushana, and Thenaali Raamakrishna, Telugu literature reached great heights under the rule of Sri Krishnadevaraya, a Vijayanagara king who was a poet himself and whose *Amukthamalyada* is as great as any other prabhandas. Srinaadha (*Kasikandam*) and Bameera Pothana (*Mahabhagavatham*) are the other important poets afterwards.

Modern Telugu Literature

Gurajada Apparao (1862–1915) is acclaimed as the epoch maker of modern Telugu literature. His magnum opus *Kanyasulkam* (1892), a play, set the tone of the future of Telugu literature. Kandukuri Veeresalingam Pantulu (1848–1919), the great social reformer, a Brahmosamaji, proclaimed that he wrote the first novel, comic play, and biography in Telugu and so he is called the Gadya Thikkana of Telugu literature. Unnava Lakshminarayana Panthulu's *Malapalli*, a novel reflecting the great ideals of the Reform movement; Mokkapati Narasinha Sasthry's *Barister Parvatheesam*, a humorous novel about a naïve young man caught in the turmoil of the East-West encounter; Gudipati Venkata Chalam's *Maidanam*, the story of the quest for freedom of a woman; and Viswanadha Satyanarayana's *Veyipadagalu*, a literary treatise upholding the values and traditions of the past, are the notable novels of the pre-Independence era.

The Novel in Telugu

The Telugu novel achieved maturity in the hands of its post-Independence writers like Kodavatiganti Kutumba Rao (*Chaduvu*), Gopichand (*Asamarthuni Jeevitha Yathra*), Buchibabu (*Chivaraku Migiledi*), Rachakonda Viswanadha Sastry (*Govulosthunnayi Jagraththa*), and Vaddera Chandi Das (*Anukshanikam*). But the Telugu novel of the 1970s and 1980s degenerated as many writers who simply exploited the popularity of journals and the vulnerability of the reading public turned out cheap romantic pot-boilers, pulp fiction, and pseudo-scientific thrillers. Kesava Reddy is one of the very few novelists who emerged during the same period swimming against the current and revitalized the Telugu novel artistically and ideologically.

Kesava Reddy: Life and Works

Born in a small village in Chittoor district, Thalapula Palli, in 1946, Kesava Reddy had his elementary and secondary education in Puthalapattu, his pre-University course in Tirupathi, and then went to Pondicherry to study Medicine. He then shifted to Dich Palli in Nizamabad district to join Victoria Hospital, a missionary hospital exclusively for the treatment of leprosy patients, and worked there till his superannuation. He now lives in Nizamabad, about 200 kilometres from Hyderabad, the capital of Andhra Pradesh.

Kesava Reddy began his literary career with the publication of a long story, *Bagavanuvacha*, in 1974. After writing two more stories, he took to novel writing and his first novel *Incredible Goddess* was published in 1977. As it is a path-breaking novel depicting the plight of the Harijans in the hands of the feudal system, it reflects not only the reasons for their ordeal but also laments their passivity and submissiveness, thereby asserting the need for a revolt by them. *Smasanam Dunneru* (1979) is almost a sequel to it. *Athadu Adavini Jayinchadu* (1984) proved that Kesava Reddy is a true avant garde writer. Its translation into English (*He Who Conquered the Jungle*, 1998) brought it the status of a modern classic. With two other novels, *City Beautiful* (1986) and *Ramudundadu, Rajjivundadi* (1987), he ensured his place in the contemporary Telugu literature. The former depicted the dehumanization of the so-called civilized cities whereas the latter stoked the beginning of the menace of globalization which uprooted traditional craftsmen. In *Chivari Gudise* (1991), he depicted the precarious conditions of marginalized peoples and *Moogavani Pillanagrovi*, the present novel, which was published in 1993 became an instant classic. Recently, he wrote a novel *Munemma* (2007) after nearly a decade.

Kesava Reddy's novel *Ballad of Ontillu* grips the reader, offering a tempo that never slackens till the end. The telling hardly allows the reader to think of its literary and sociological implications. Like great novelists of different times, places, and languages, Kesava Reddy knows that the fundamental duty of a novelist is to tell a plausible story. He seems to have learnt the alchemy of relating the same story again and again from the folk artists of Chittoor district without slackening the tempo and rhythm. The childhood he spent in the villages of the region, the erstwhile north Arcot district of pre-Independence India, acquainted him with not only the Ramayana and the Mahabharata but also ballads like *Kavamma Katha*, *Kaatamaraayudi Katha*, and *Mugguru Maraateelu* sung through the night till noon to the next day to an enthralled audience. It is because the reader thrills to Kesava Reddy's novels that he/she misses the literary strategies behind the novels. Thus, Kesava Reddy's novels prove the maxim that art disappears in great works of art.

MADHURANTHAKAM NARENDRA

A Literary Overview of Ontillu

It is a very strange feeling one has in undertaking any introduction to Kesava Reddy's novella and that is for two reasons: first, it is undoubtedly a master work in its genre; and second, because of its profound relevance to what must be one of the most intense and agonizing issues in India at this moment.

As for the first matter – the sheer power of its literary force – the only serious test is of course in the reading, and I do not hesitate to advise the reader to turn immediately to the work itself to experience the undiluted 'shock of recognition'. The more disarmed, the more defenseless one is, the better, not least because of the role the reader (better to say, the listener) must play in the creative realization of the story's significance as it lays open its own distress, which is the distress of India itself, specifically regarding the land proper and how it is to be held. With what kind of consciousness is the holding of that land to be understood? It is impossible to think anyone could own it. But to be disarmed, to make oneself defenseless, does not mean to be ignorant of either the current strife or the five thousand years' of accumulation of memory and custom. The more one knows of India and the more deeply one senses what that knowing is, the more the reader is rewarded. This of course is where I, very much a 'stranger from afar' here on the cold granite coast of Nova Scotia, most feel my inadequacy and temerity in speaking of the *Ballad of Ontillu*.

Since nothing is drearier, more distorting, or more joy-killing for the reader than to be offered a plot-summary or a skeletal synopsis, I will refrain. In any event, the story seems to direct its own reading; a voice begins to talk and one is immediately engaged as a listener, involved in the business of determining the meaning and import of certain curious monuments and practices, including the presence of a haunting, uncanny, small wilderness of dense forest growth, known as Bakkireddy Thicket, at one of the entry paths to a village called Ontillu or One House. The name itself, that narrating voice suggests, is a bit puzzling since there are clearly more than one, in fact as many as two hundred hearths. It must be said of Ontillu, as Melville said of Queequeg's island of Kokovoro in *Moby Dick*, 'It is not drawn in any map; true places never are'. The story of Ontillu is the story of how that forest came to exist, and why despite the obvious utility it might have for the villagers, as much in need as any other rural place for firewood and saw logs, it remains eternally untouched in its protective uncanniness. This story, which forms the material that is shaped in the intricate architecture of Reddy's novella in its brevity and poetic (or formal) clarity, achieves classic statement. A great part of its creativity lies in the self-reflective construction, as if it were constantly new by virtue of the way it builds up its subtle repetitions and mirrorings – the mythic dimension is always present, giving the sense of 'facts' transforming or transcending, metamorphosing into legend, and becoming something truer and finer, because more philosophical, than history. There is an experience of speed and purity, with nothing extraneous or merely willed into being. In the swift, deft presentation of images, its 'scenario', if you will – Reddy is a master of composition by scene – there is almost nothing that one does not *see* and take sense and understanding from. But because the aesthetic vehicle is language, what one sees is also shadowed by the deeper resonances possible to verbal art: the way words incorporate their own history or point to some iconic allusion. The etymology of 'tahasildar', for instance, with its roots in Persian and Arabic, reflects significant epochs of Indian economic and social history, intricately pertinent to the depth of this account. Bakkireddy's insistent desire to be buried under a peepal tree in land, once the holding of his father and himself but forfeited forever to settle a catastrophic debt, is not fortuitous. It does not hurt one's understanding to recall the opening verses of a section of the Bhagavad Gita:

The Blessed One said:
With roots aloft and branches below,
The eternal peepal tree, they say –
Whose leaves are the Vedic hymns,
Who knows it, he knows the Veda.

In good writing, these things do not happen by mistake.

On its surface or purely narrative level, one might say for the sake of economy that *Ballad of Ontillu* is the record of how the village comes to effect a satisfactory explanation of a seemingly bizarre, unnatural instance of an all-too-common and ordinary event. Goethe asked, 'What is a *Novelle* about but an event which is unheard of but has taken place?' In Ontillu, the people know from the Village Administrator to the porter of the Council

Office that 'many and varied were the ways a farmer can die'. All of India knows that, and more horribly knows how many hundreds of thousands die, year after year.

> Yes, they had seen or heard of all that and more. But Bakkireddy was the first and only time they saw with their own eyes a farmer who, ploughing land which had been sold off in auction and no longer his, overcome by exhaustion, collapses in the furrow he was making and breathes his last. They remembered the great tranquillity and serenity of that face looking up from the flooded furrow. And why not? After all it was his own land that he lay in, and his own plough handle that his left hand held and his own driving stick that was in his right. It was with this knowledge that he breathed his last, tranquil and serene.

This odd, unexpected peripety is the heart of the book. Bankrupt, insane, and suicidal; yet the man dies somehow blessed. At least the reader sees that; the villagers believe they have seen a farmer as obsessed with his land as they know of the obsessions of Duryodhana for power and of Yudhishtira's for truth and are made melancholic and despondent in consequence. Nonetheless, the rains in which Bakkireddy died have filled the tanks and wells; the land is fertile and prosperous; slowly the memory of Bakkireddy's story begins to fade. But only to be brought back suddenly and violently by a further catastrophe that occurs on that land, now the property belonging to the Village Administrator. The second sad event at 'Roadside Land' is even more mysterious than the manner of Bakkireddy's death. When I say 'mysterious', I do not mean the stuff of detective novels, though that element is not missing, but rather that the *real* of art can never be the 'reality' of the positivist. Needing an answer to that mystery, since he is now himself the victim of the second catastrophe, the Village Administrator sets everything in his life aside in order to lead a most earnest and driven quest for the truth of who or what caused his three prized cows to simultaneously abort their calves on the rich grass growing near the mound of Bakkireddy's grave under the peepal tree in the fallow lands that had once been his. After a long, heroic, and slightly comic campaign, the result is not a forensic demonstration of established fact but the fabrication of a small, rather beautiful myth. It satisfies the Village Administrator; it satisfies his relatives, his friends, and his well-wishers. It is adopted by Ontillu and becomes central to its history and geography; since the Five Elements themselves declare Bakkireddy a Karmayogi and the 'Roadside Land' eternally his.

But will it satisfy the reader? Perhaps that is the wrong question. Like all myths, the myth that grows up around the ordeal of Bakkireddy has its veridical core: it is the vital, eternal question of social justice. Denied the hope implied in that question, the human project is a dead letter. In retrospect, Reddy's book is of the kind that rewards many readings, one of its most brilliant passages being a seemingly incidental episode that makes up most of the Chapter 'Harischandra'. An actor, who was to play the role of the king in *'Saythya Harischandra'*, a play which, in the drought, the villagers had chosen to put on in the hope of appeasing the heavens, wanders back 'like a hungry dog looking for food' to the abandoned shack that had been used for rehearsals. Now a man with his occupation gone, since the rains had fallen according to heaven's strange way of doing what it will when it will and cancelling the need for the play to be performed, he recalls his repeatedly failed attempts during the rehearsals to find in his face or voice the adequate expression of pathos for his Queen's suffering. 'Today, however, seated on the pyol, the actor inadvertently called mind the left hand holding the plough handle, the right holding the cattle-prod, and the body lying, half-submerged, in the water and, lo, unprompted, tears welled up in his eyes and ran down his cheeks.' There is no further comment or elaboration. Possibly, for the reader in India, nothing more needs to be said. The folkloric, spontaneous originality that so much characterizes this book depends on the masterful way the author works with the *unsaid*, those silently shared, known, always accompanying awareness, 'enthymemes' (things located in the heart or mind to use the term of the great Russian critic and theorist, Mikhail Bakhtin) that make up the cultural consciousness of a community. The allusion to this play is what grounds the unspoken direction of Reddy's novel and teaches us how to read the myth of Bakkireddy's Thicket. I think we can say that we have heard of the play somewhere before.

> This play – Harischandra – captured my heart. I could never be tired of seeing it. ... It haunted me and I must have acted Harischandra to myself times without number. 'Why should not all be truthful like Harischandra?' was the question I asked myself day and night. To follow truth and to go through all the ordeals Harischandra went through was the one ideal it inspired in me.
>
> – Mahatma Gandhi,
> *The Story of My Experiments with Truth*

I do not think it was ever Reddy's intention to make Mahatma Gandhi in anyway necessary to comprehending his own work. 'Gandhi', if you will, is simply part of the Indian consciousness, part of its myriad-figured repertoire of divine, semi-divine, and human personages.

Firm allegiance to truth, to the need for social justice and steadfastness in the truth, are the shared elements.

Ballad of Ontillu is a work of art, a work of the moral imagination appealing deeply to our moral imagination, where it is realized according to our need for it. And at the moment that need is great. 'We trust to novels to train us in the practice of great indignations and great generosities' was the faith of Henry James. Reddy's work honours that practice. William James, the great psychologist and brother of the novelist, wrote, '"Will you or won't you have it so", is the most pressing question we are ever asked.' *Ballad of Ontillu* helps us to face that question.

J.K. SNYDER

Prologue

My village is called Ontillu, that is One House. The name is misleading; the village consists of no less than two hundred hearths. It lies to the east of the Chittor-Cuddapah State Highway, more or less at the 34-kilometre marker. The east end of the village abuts a mountain range, which bars any entrance from that direction. There are, however, paths leading to it from the three other directions. Were you to approach from the south, you would come across a curious sight. There, at the very portal of the village, you would see a huge rock some 20 feet high and shaped like an egg standing on its broader. And you would notice on it three vertical stripes, the middle one red and the other two white. A priest would be standing below it bowing and offering prayers. The sight of a priest worshipping a big rock might well surprise you, but you would only have to question him or one of the devotees worshipping with him there for an explanation. The reply whether from priest or devotee would be the same:

'This, O stranger from afar, is called Hanuman Rock. Long, long ago a great battle took place between Rama and Ravana. During the fighting Lachmana was wounded and fell into a swoon, whereupon Hanuman went off immediately to fetch Sanjeevi Mountain.* Now Sanjeevi Mountain was no ordinary mountain. It was a hundred leagues in length and just as many in breadth, swaddled in thick woods and ravines. All manner of wild beasts roamed its sides. That's the sort of mountain Hanuman managed to tear up and hoist to his shoulder and then soar off into the sky with. As he flew and flew he grew more and more weary, for the journey was long and arduous. And just as he was passing here, here, right above our village he was so overwhelmed by fatigue that he paused, flew down, and rested one of his big toes on

---

* A legendary mountain, referred to in Ramayana. In the battle between Rama and Ravana, Lachmana, brother of Rama, swooned. Hanuman rescued Lachmana by fetching the Sanjeevi Mountain, rich in life-saving herbs.

this rock for a fraction of a second to recover his breath. Lo, at the very touch of his toe, the rock became sacred.

   'It must be said in all fairness that not only Lakshmana but Rama, too, was rescued from sure death ever so many times by Hanuman. Ramayana can perhaps live without Rama but certainly not without Hanuman. That Hanuman out of all the places in this vast country should choose to pause and rest here testifies that ours is one of the most blessed of villages. Having turned to our village for his relief, he encircled it with his giant tail to protect it the way the nail protects the toe. We worship at Hanuman Rock every day and observe Hanuman Festival each year in the month of April.'

* * *

If you were to approach the village from the north, you would come upon another intriguing thing: a temple set on the embankment of an agricultural water tank. It is a shrine, so small that if you stood beside it, it would hardly come up to your waist. The shrine does not have a compound wall, a temple spire, or a flagmast. Its walls are stone and a large slab of rock serves for its roof. Inside sits a female idol carved out of black stone, her face besmeared with turmeric, her forehead touched with vermilion. Surely finding a small temple perched on the embankment of a water tank would be a cause for surprise, but you would only have to ask the man

sitting there with his fishing rod or the woman gathering
mushrooms on the embankment slope and either would
explain, 'This, O traveller from afar, is called Chinamma
Temple. Long, long ago, about two generations ago,
a chieftain governed this province. It was he indeed
who got this water tank constructed. Whether the
hour for the construction to begin was auspicious or
not, no one knows. But just as the tank was brimming
and the water was ready to spill into the sluice, lo, the
embankment collapsed completely, causing a huge
breach at its midpoint, and the entire mass of water
flooded out, not a single drop remained in the tank.'
The chieftain called back the tank-diggers and ordered
the embankment redone. Once again it collapsed. And
the chieftain, not the man to give in easily, ordered it to
be rebuilt, with the same result. He had it redone ten
times or more but, alas, it collapsed just as many times.
Some years passed in this futile exercise. Neither the
chieftain nor the tank-diggers could understand what
would cause the embankment to cave in as it did. At
last the exasperated chieftain, on a certain Friday, having
asked for a priest to honour and propitiate the goddess
Gangamma, implored her, 'O, great mother, why is the
embankment caving in like this? Kindly make it known
to me what my sin was, what my crime was!' Gangamma,
holy mother, possessed the priest and through him

proclaimed, 'O child, it is not for you to ask me questions. Listen – I am going to tell you what you must do to keep the embankment. Bury a girl, a virgin, alive in the breach. The sacrifice will ensure the soundness of the embankment.'

'Upon hearing the decree, the chieftain's heart sank. If only it were an old hag or a jade, he would get around to carrying it out, one way or another. But to bury a young virgin in the breach and she still alive! He was after all the headman of the province. If he so much as issued an order that such and such a man's daughter be brought along and cast into the breach, the order would be carried out in a flash. But how and when would that sin be atoned? On the other hand, the land lying below the tank became more and more parched and remained uncultivated for years. The people were wailing for water and grain. 'O God! What am I to do,' said the chieftain and took to his bed. His grief was so great that for days on end he stayed so, refusing all food and drink and hardly speaking to anyone.

Then Chinamma, his youngest daughter of marriageable age, went to him and asked, 'Why do you grieve O father? Does it become a chieftain to lie in bed when his subjects are crying out for food and water? Are you the fosterer of your subjects or their tormenter? Get up and do as goddess Gangamma bade you. Take me to the embankment and bury me in the breach. Do not counter my word, for I have made up my mind to be the sacrifice. Please see to the arrangements needed for that!' The sorrow of the chieftain can only be imagined. How was he to bring himself to bury the girl he had fathered, the girl he was to marry off, after washing her bridegroom's feet? But Chinamma was adamant; her decision was as firm as the grip of guano. The chieftain pleaded with her to change her mind. He threatened and beseeched her. Chinamma was unrelenting. He wept and wailed and sulked – all to no avail. Then he went to the Brahmin, and the Brahmin fixed the day and the propitious hour.

'On that day, Chinamma had a bath and burnished her hair with fragrant oil. She clothed herself in a silk sari and a silk blouse, then decked herself from head to toe with gold ornaments. She was lifted into the howdah on an elephant's back and taken in procession, just like a bride. Musicians playing clarinets and beating drums led the procession. Women of good omen carrying large shining bronze trays loaded with piles of turmeric, vermilion, camphor, and flowers brought up the rear. As the procession inched along, the people who lined both sides of the street wept openly, their tears falling like heavy rain to the earth. When the procession finally made it to the embankment, Chinamma descended from the howdah. Staring past the great crowd of people who had gathered and were beating their foreheads in their grief, propelled by her iron determination, she climbed down into the breach and sat cross-legged there. She ordered the tank-diggers to level the breach, then joined her palms together and closed her eyes. There was a look of great tranquillity on her face. The tank diggers took up their spades and began to shovel the mud and gravel into the breach, pausing only to wipe away their blinding tears. And that was the last we ever saw Chinamma. The embankment never caved in again. And there where Chinamma had sat, this temple arose. Every Friday we make offerings to her and in August every year we hold her Festival.'

* * *

Now if you were to enter the village from the west, you would have yet another strange experience. There, adjoining the road and only a short distance from the centre of the village – no more than shouting distance – you'd come across a large and tall thicket filled with trees of all varieties, many of them precious ones like banyan, fig, sal, and peepal, to name only a few. The trunks are huge and the limbs branch and divide and re-divide reaching up almost into the clouds. Thick creepers spread and climb up the trunks entwining everything everywhere giving the whole grove a wild and uncanny appearance. Anyone seeing it for the first time cannot avoid shivering and feeling their hair rise at its strangeness. You would also wonder that such a forest, so short a distance from a village of two hundred hearths, was untouched. But you'd only have to ask the boy driving cattle on the road, or the girl going along behind them gathering cow dung to tell you something about it. They both would answer in the same way.

'This, O pilgrim from afar, is called Bakkireddy Thicket. About thirty years ago, there lived in the village a farmer by the name of Bakkireddy. A righteous and honest man, we remember him every evening when we light the lamp at dusk. He never lived off another man's suffering or caused another man sorrow. He lived by the sweat of his own labour. He owned five acres of land, which were at once his soul and the sustainer of that soul. And of course, as you know, it is only the good like him that misfortune pursues. When he got so old he could only walk with the help of a stick, that dark star Saturn sat on his head. He found himself up to the neck in debt. The bank people sent a notice that he had to pay off all his loans and their interest. But the poor man was down and out. And you know bank people. They sent reminder after reminder and finally a notice that the land would have to be put up for auction. The auction notice was pasted on the door of Bakkireddy's house and on the door of the Village Panchayath Office;* it was published in all the local newspapers.

And on the date set, the bank people came along in a jeep. The jeep entered the village when the sun was only two fathoms high in the eastern sky....

* Village Council Office.

The Dispossessed

The jeep entered the village when the sun was two fathoms high. It negotiated its way through the streets and pulled up in front of the Village Panchayath Office. And by the time the sun had risen to about four fathoms high, it was all over. The auction was executed, and Bakkireddy's land was sold off. The documents pertaining to the sale were prepared. Bakkireddy signed as the seller of the land; the Maniam* signed as the purchaser. The Karanam** and two others from the village signed as witnesses to the sale. The

* Village Administrator. Maniam collects land taxes from the farmers. He is also responsible for law and order in the village.

** Village Accountant. Karanam maintains various registers and documents pertaining to landed property of the villagers. He also functions as land surveyor.

State official who supervised the auction put down his signature in English. The junior clerk affixed a seal under the State officer's signature and marked it with a rubber stamp. Then the officer rather solemnly and personally handed one copy of the document to the seller and one to the purchaser. Each document was rolled up into a scroll and securely tied with a white cotton thread, for they were of great legal value. The junior clerk gathered up the registers, files, and other paraphernalia, and stowed them in the jeep. The State officer climbed in. The jeep grunted to a start, then swayed, and lumbered its way back through the streets to the State Highway.

The Maniam emerged from the Village Panchayath Office holding the scroll of the sale document in one hand and the edge of his dhoti in the other. He walked across the street, mounted his horse that stood under a neem tree, and rode off in the direction of his house. The Karanam lit his cigar and went off in the opposite direction. The other two witnesses walked along beside him trying to engage him in conversation. One by one the people who had come to participate in the auction or just to watch it, drifted away.

When everyone had left, the Thalari* stepped out of the council room, took off his turban, and dropped it to

* Village Servant. These are traditionally held posts paid by State. The Thalari assists the aforementioned village officials.

the floor, then sat on it and lit a beedi. He smoked two of them, one right after the other. He lit a third, took a few puffs, then noticed that the sun was nearing mid-sky. He put out the beedi, stuck it behind his ear, and stood up. He carried the table, chairs, and benches from the corridor back into the Council Room and was about to padlock the door when he noticed a man sitting all hunched over in the far corner. Very slowly he walked over to him.

In the darkened corner of the room, Bakkireddy was sitting on the floor motionless and absorbed. The scrolled document lay in his lap. The caretaker bent forward and asked, 'Ah, I see, Ayya is still here. Do you want to rest here for a little while, Ayya?'

Bakkireddy lifted his face and said meekly, 'No, friend, I…I would rather go home.' He held the scroll in his left hand and with the other pushed himself up, first against the floor and then against his knee. As he rose his knees and hips creaked loud enough to be heard. He had been sitting for a long time and the sudden rise made him feel faint and wobbly. His body shook and he staggered when he took his first steps as if he were about to fall. But the Thalari steadied him. Bakkireddy moved as if he was wading in knee-deep water, holding himself up with the support of the wall and doorframe and stepped out into the corridor. By then, the sinking feeling had left him.

There was no one in the street in front of the
Panchayath Office. It was littered with stubs of beedis
and cigars and scattered matchsticks left by the auction
crowd. Bakkireddy climbed down the steps and set
out along the street towards his house. His gait was
awkward, as if the tendons in his ankles had been cut.
A herd of cattle was moving down the street, coming
towards him. A cowherd walked behind them holding
a bamboo cane. Bakkireddy moved to the side of the
street to make way for them. One of the cows stopped
in the middle of the street, turned her neck, and mooed.
'Get going, you!' the cowherd shouted. 'What do you
mean by standing right in the middle of the road and
mooing like that? You think you're the only one that's
ever had a calf?' The cane in his hand smacked her flank.
The cow swished her tail and brushed her flank, then
mooed again, still louder. The cowherd shouted again,
'Who's going to steal your calf? Some thief from Cotton
Mountain? Get going. Can't you see the sun is near
mid-sky?' He whacked her again on the other flank.
She straightened her neck and started jogging down the
street, her tail flopping about, and her milk-heavy udder
swinging beneath her.

After the cows had passed, Bakkiredddy moved back
into the middle of the street and resumed his walk. His
gait was much more awkward now, as if the tendons in

his knees as well as in his ankles were cut. Really, he looked like a dried up banana leaf being driven by the wind hither and thither down the street. He reached his house more by drifting than walking. And when he got there, he didn't go in. Instead he went into his cattleshed, which was adjacent to the house. The shed was a post and beam structure with a grass-thatched roof. It had mud walls on three sides and was open on the fourth. Inside, a pair of tethered bulls lay at their stakes chewing cud. There was still a layer of paddy grass in the manger. Various agricultural implements like plough handles, yokes, hoes, etc., leaned against the walls or hung from pegs. Towards one end of the shed was a spring cot. Wearily Bakkireddy walked up to it and dropped on the springs. He sat there with his back against the wall. He took the rolled-up document of sale, pushed his right index finger behind the cotton thread, and pulled it with a certain amount of force. It broke with a soft snap.

* * *

I pushed my right index finger behind my father's waist thread and pulled it with a certain amount of force. It broke with a soft snap. That was the first time I ever touched a dead body. Strange! I had no idea that after death a body would turn so cold. My father's body was as cold as a grinding stone drenched in dew. My uncle came along pushing his way through the

crowd that was gathering around the dead body and
began giving me instructions, one after the other. He
handed me a wisp of paddy grass. I placed my father's
big toes together and tied them with the paddy grass.
My uncle put a rupee in my palm. I dropped the coin
into my father's mouth, which was agape. His face
looked sad and melancholic with the mouth open like
that. I wanted to close it shut and started to push the
chin up. Incredible! Another thing I hadn't known till
that moment was that parts of the body would stiffen
so much after death. I needed all my strength to push
the mouth completely closed. Then it looked solemn
and grave. The eyes were still and gazed up at the
ridgepole of the house. They didn't sparkle, nor did
the ridgepole reflect in them. I pushed the lids down
over the eyeballs. My uncle fetched a wattle basket and
placed it upside down near the head of the corpse. A
woman put a clay saucer containing oil and a cotton
wick on the basket. My uncle handed me a matchbox.
I struck a match, lit the oil lamp, then went round, and
stood at the feet of the corpse with my palms pressed
together. At that point, the wailing began. The people
in the room started weeping one after the other, one by
one consoling or being consoled. As for me, I did not
cry. My eyes remained dry until the bier to carry away
my father's body was ready.

They made the bier out of green bamboo poles. First, they wrapped the body from the neck to the feet in white linen, then lifted it and placed it on the bier. The men tied the body to the bier with hand-twisted paddy grass rope, pulling it with all their strength as they passed the rope over and over my father's neck, chest, stomach, waist, thighs, knees, and ankles and knotted it securely to the bier. Then and only then it came through to me that my father was no more. Never again would he get up or hold the plough handle in his left hand or the cattle driving stick in his right. And at last the tears burst forth from my eyes that had been dry until then. My jaws quivered with the sobbing I could not control; my chest heaved and fell in my grief.

The Scroll

Bakkireddy threw away the cotton thread. He unrolled the document and tried to spread it open out on his lap. But the scroll would not oblige him. As a matter of fact, it rebelled and behaved like a living thing with a will of its own. When he managed to keep the top of the scroll more or less flat, the lower part would bounce about and curl up on its own accord. And when he tried to deal with the lower part and keep it stretched out, the top would shake itself and roll up. He looked at the scroll for a long time contemptuously as if it were an adversary. He was amazed at what seemed to be the insolence and impudence of the lifeless object in his lap. Finally, using the fingers of both hands, he managed to pin it down on his lap and began to read the contents.

Deed of Sale

This Deed of Sale is made and executed on this day the 28th day of June, 1950, equivalant of 2nd of Ashad month. Sri Kadati Bakkireddy son of Kadati Rangareddy, aged 60 years, agriculturist, native of Ontillu village, Chittoor district and Chittoor taluq, here in after called the vendor of the property which term shall mean and include all his heirs, Executors, Administrators, Legal Representatives, Nominees, Successors in interest, and assignees, etc., in favour of Sri Midde Dorai Swami Reddy, son of Midde Kumara Swami Reddy, aged 54 years, village administrator, native of Ontillu village, Chittoor district and Chittoor taluq, here in after called the vendee of the property which term shall mean and include all the heirs, Executors, Administrators, Legal Representatives, Nominees, Successor in interest and assignees, etc., whereas the vendor here in is the sole and absolute owner and peaceful possessor of the scheduled property.

And whereas the vendor, due to personal needs and family necessities has offered and agreed to sell the scheduled property to the vendee for a sale consideration of Rs. 24000/- (twenty-four thousands only) and the vendee has agreed to purchase the same.

Now the deed of sale witnesseth as follows

In pursuance of the said sale consideration of Rs. 24000/- the vendor has received the above said amount from the vendee by way of cash and the vendor hereby admits and acknowledges the receipt of the said sum and also puts the vendee in actual and physical possession of the scheduled property described in the schedule here under.

The vendor has today delivered to the vendee vacant, physical and peaceful possession and enjoyment of the scheduled property assuring such peaceful possession and enjoyment forever the vendor hereby declares that the vendee shall be absolutely entitled to hold and enjoy the scheduled property as the rightful, sole and absolute owner and can enjoy all the privileges, facilities, easements, advantages and appurtenants here to whatsoever to the scheduled property and any parts thereof without any let or hindrance either from the vendor or from anyone claiming through the vendor and to the entire exclusion of the vendee forever.

Schedule of the Property

Agricultural land that goes by the name of 'Roadside Land', wet land, 5 acres in extent, survey numbers 179, 180, 181 and 182 located on the outskirts of Ontillu village, Chittoor district and Chittoor taluq:

Boundaries

> *West: Chittoor to Cuddapah State Highway*
> *East: Pakala Subba Reddy's land*
> *North: Galla Narasimha Naidu's land*
> *South: Big river*
> *In witness whereof the vendor has signed on this Deed of Sale with his own free will and consent on this day, month and year first mentioned above ...*

Bakkireddy could not bear to read any further. A thick layer of tears clouded his eyes and through those clouds he could see his father's face.

* * *

Never could my father have thought of his land as a commodity to be bought or sold at will. Most surely the notion that the land was endowed with vital, mental, and even spiritual elements real as its physical being had been ingrained in him. He treated his land as if it were as much a part of himself as his wife and children, his relatives, his neighbours. He was rather young – not more than forty years old – when he passed away. I do remember that his death came about during a certain summer. He had been bedridden for nearly six months. The illness started with a paralysis of his legs and hands. A few weeks later, he lost control of his lips and tongue; his breathing became laboured and irregular. In time, it was all too clear to him what his real state was. He asked that the relatives be sent for; they all lived in villages within ten to twelve kilometres of our own. As soon as the message reached them, my relatives got ready to come to us. It was summer, so they were not so busy farming their land. My maternal uncle arrived with his whole family. The relatives gathered around my father's bed and inquired after him. As they spoke many were wiping their eyes with the sari-end or an upper cloth, but despite all the tears, my father's remained dry. The relatives filed out one by one. When everyone had left the room, my father gestured to me to call my uncle back in.

My uncle came in and asked, 'What is it, brother-in-law?'

My father was lying on his back with his face turned to a side. He kept gazing fixedly at my uncle's face.

'Did you ask me to come in, brother-in-law? What is it you want of me?'

But my father only continued to gaze at him. He did intend to say a hundred, a thousand things. His lips and tongue moved awkwardly, but he couldn't form any word. My uncle came closer to the cot.

'Why do you grieve?' he asked. 'What will be shall be. Your grieving will not change a thing, will it?'

My father was still making an effort to speak about what troubled him. My uncle sat on the frame of the cot. 'You live such a righteous life that you are held in the highest esteem by one and all in the village. Did you know that? ... Yes, it is true. People will remember you every time they light their lamps at dusk. And what more can you ask for, brother-in-law?'

A violent fit of coughing came over my father. It seemed as if all his troubles were choking him. His eyes were wild. He coughed for a long time. Then my uncle said, 'Brother-in-law, you have a worthy son. He will lead a righteous life, just as you did. Whichever way you look at it, there is no reason for you to grieve.'

My father took his eyes off my uncle and stared at me for a long while. But in the end he shook his head in disapproval.

Then uncle took my father's hand into his and said, 'You own five acres of land by the roadside. The land is so fertile; each acre is worth its weight in diamonds.' He pointed his finger at me and added, 'And your son here will take over the land and....'

At that point all of a sudden my father's eyes flitted back and forth like a fish caught on a hook, his eyelid fluttered like a bird caught in a net. His face twisted in pain as if pierced by poisonous thorns. Somehow he mustered just enough strength to whisper, 'Land ... land ... he must keep the land.' And as he said 'land' his eyes grew moist and in the moisture there were pools of tears. My uncle grasped him by the shoulders, 'Why would he not keep the land? – If need be he would put his finger in the mouth of a black cobra. But the land he would never lose. Is that all you are worried about, brother-in-law?'

My father, still only able to speak in a faltering voice, said, 'I will be gone in a day or two. But my soul will always be upon my land. And my son ... he cannot tell east from west. He – he is only a child....' But he wasn't able to complete his thought; the words wouldn't come, and he was overcome by a great fatigue.

'Come now, brother-in-law,' my uncle sighed, a mild anger in his voice, 'What kind of child is he? Great procrastinator that you are, you didn't get him married in time, or he would have a son or two himself by now.'

Then he pulled me close to the cot and said, 'Speak up, boy, is it you who will let the land go?' I came up very close to the cot – so close my knees touched the wooden frame. I could see that my father was not in the least comforted by what my uncle had said. I knew he was yearning, longing for a word, a promise, a guarantee, an assurance from me. So I looked straight into his eyes, took a deep breath, and said in a firm, forceful voice,

'Father, I will keep the land. Of course I will. I will protect the land like the eyelid protects the eye. I am a farmer's son, not a vagabond.'

How old was I at that time? I don't know. But I remember, I had not yet begun to visit the barber shop to have my beard shaved. When my father heard the words and saw the way I spoke them, he was greatly relieved. He took a deep breath and exhaled it slowly. His whole body seemed to relax. The tears stopped and his eyes were the picture of tranquillity.

That night my father fell into a coma. Since it seemed doubtful that he would recover, the relatives who had come from the outlying villages postponed their departure. Ours was a small house, but it was no inconvenience for us to accommodate them all. Two huge tamarind trees sheltered the front of the house and the relatives rolled out date leaf mats and slept on them at night.

In the small hours of the third day, my father breathed his last.

The Peepal Tree

Bakkireddy had the sale document stretched out and pinned down against his lap. His eyes were riveted on the sentence: 'The vendor has today delivered to the vendee

vacant, physical, and peaceful possession and enjoyment
of the scheduled property assuring such peaceful
possession and enjoyment forever.' He fancied that each
letter in the sentence was growing in size by degrees and
the letters were turning into boulders and that he himself
was being buried under them. He stretched his neck and
shook his head as if to avoid being suffocated. In the
process he let go of the document, which quickly rolled
itself back up into a scroll. He looked for the cotton
thread he had snapped off, wanting to tie up the scroll
again, but could not find it in the cot or underneath it.
Perhaps the wind had blown it away. He got up off the
cot and found a bit of paddy grass from the manger and
tied it around the scroll. Then he put it in a wall-niche
directly opposite and lay down again on the cot. He laid
there, his hands behind his head, keeping an eye on the
niche. The niche was dark and the white parchment
showed distinctly in the darkness. The gaze was intense
and unflinching, his field of vision shrank and shrank
until he could see nothing but the white scroll of the
document in the niche. And then he couldn't distinguish
between the white scroll of the document and the
linen-wrapped corpse of his father.

* * *

My father's corpse had been wrapped in white linen
from the neck down to his feet. They placed him on

the bier and secured the body with hand-twisted paddy grass ropes. Three men on either side of the bier lifted it and bore it on their shoulders. As they raised the bier, the people standing by rent the air with their chant, GOVINDA! GOVINDA! At the same time the drums began to thunder. But I heard neither the chanting nor the drumming. I was sobbing unconsolably. My uncle came up to me and handed me an earthen pitcher containing live coals. He patted me on the shoulder for a while and then rushed away.

My father's last journey began as a procession. I trailed behind the bier and the bearers, wiping away tears with my left hand and holding the ropes of the earthen pitcher in my right. The procession passed down the streets, crossed the western boundary of the village, through the tamarind grove and the aloe hedges, and came to a halt by our Roadside Land. Near the south limit of our land there stood a very tall peepal tree. Beyond the peepal tree the river flowed. It ran full only in the rainy season. After the rainy season, it dwindled to a small narrow stream gurgling over the stones. Between the river and the peepal tree was a narrow strip of heath. There a grave had been dug, which was to be my father's last resting place. The bier was lowered at the edge of the grave.

It had taken the procession a very long time to get to the gravesite. In the first place, for some reason, the bearers had moved at a snail's pace, even though the sun beat down fiercely. And then they stopped for an hour on the way. I never understood why. But once we arrived at Roadside Land, things moved forward in quick succession. They removed the paddy grass ropes binding the corpse and broke them into tiny bits. The green bamboo poles used for the bier were chopped up, too, and the bits of rope and poles were thrown into nearby cork tree bushes. Then the earthen pitcher was taken from me and smashed into a thousand pieces. All this was carried out I was to learn later in observance of the custom that every article that accompanied the corpse should be rendered completely unfit for any further use. The corpse, still wrapped in its white linen was lowered into the pit. Two people who had climbed down into the pit were waiting at the bottom of the grave to arrange the body with its head to the south. When my uncle nodded to me, I let the mud in my cupped hands stream down on the corpse. Three times. I couldn't remember on what part of the body the mud fell. The pit was very dark at the bottom. Everything was indistinct except for the low white glow of the linen. And then the elders in the crowd set about pushing mud into the pit, some with spades, some with their cupped hands. As I watched, the pit was filled and levelled. Now, my father was buried. On the grave, they heaped the earth up into a mound about a cubit high and planted a basil sapling on top of it. Each morning I used to fetch water from the river and water it. In two days the sapling had sunk its roots and lifted up its head. After watering it I used to crouch down and watch the sapling grow tall, throwing out new shoots, which turned into leaves and buds and then into flowers.

The Bat

Bakkireddy lay on his back, his palms beneath his head, staring at the wall-niche and the scrolled up document in it. He was struck by the likeness of the white document to his father's wrapped corpse. He found himself muttering, 'This morning, by selling my land at auction, I buried my father a second time.' He half rose from the cot on his elbow with the intention of getting up and retrieving the scroll. But at that moment, he heard a familiar noise in the loft of the cattleshed. A bat that lived in the loft darted out and began flying in circles. Bakkireddy dropped back on the cot as if someone had pushed him down. He lay there watching the creature and listening to the flutter of its wings with some curiosity and interest. All of a sudden the bat made a thin screeching noise and hurled itself into the wall-niche. The scrolled document fell to the ground with a thud. With a start Bakkireddy sat up. Only then did he notice that he was perspiring profusely and had been for some time. Sweat poured from every pore in his body. And he was thirsty. He got up from the cot and started to go to the kitchen of his house where they stored water. As he passed through the courtyard he noticed his wife sitting, leaning against some bags of grain. She had a fold of her sari in her mouth attempting to muffle a sob. Two women sat with her entreating her in low voices. Bakkireddy did not stop, but moved on towards the kitchen. There he dipped an aluminium tumbler into the pot, threw back his head, and gulped the water. Some of it escaped from the corners of his mouth and ran down his chin and neck. He stooped and dipped the tumbler in for a second drink. As he gulped it down, he heard his wife let out an unearthly scream. He turned and looked towards the courtyard. Her shriek had turned into a moaning wail. She had let her sari-end fall and was beating her breasts. Even as the other women watched helplessly, she dropped to the ground, wailing and rolling in the chaff. A rooster that had been raking through the chaff looking for seeds stopped in its search and stretched out its neck in bewilderment. Then it flew up clumsily with a great flopping of wings and cackling noises to the top of the courtyard wall and dropped down on the other side, cackling even louder, and disappeared. Bakkireddy let the tumbler slip out of his hand and drop into the water pot. He straightened his back and walked quickly out of the kitchen to the centre of the courtyard. There he stopped and stood silently, his hands hanging loosely at his sides, like a criminal, like one who was confessing to his crime and accepting his punishment. He stood there like that for a while, then looked up lifting his face to the sky and scratched his neck with both hands. Slowly, as if he was counting his steps, he walked back to the cattle shed and lay down again on the cot. His heart was pounding hard against his chest wall.

How surprising! He had never thought his wife could cry so terribly or so hysterically. She had been married to him for nearly forty years. In all that long time he had seen her face many trials and tribulations and take them all in her stride with remarkable endurance and stoicism. It had been his experience that she would cry until her eyes came to resemble live coals and then she would silently pine away. Even a person sitting next to her would not be aware of her suffering. In her grief she would refuse food and drink for days on end and would not knot her hair for weeks. But never until today had he seen her cry so loudly or in such a hysterical manner. And the moaning and wailing in the courtyard could still be heard in the cattleshed.

* * *

My mother let out a blood-curdling scream. The scream turned into a moaning and wailing and she began to beat her breasts. That was on the tenth-day ceremony* of my father's death. A large number of relations and friends turned up on that day. The crowd was much larger than the one that had attended the burial service. By the time the sun was four fathoms high, all of us had gathered at Roadside Land. On that day, my mother and I were required to carry out ever so many rituals at my father's grave. Most of the rituals I have either forgotten completely or could remember only vaguely. But some of them I do remember vividly and to the last detail even now because they affected me deeply as I performed them. Thus, it happened that on that day the village barber sat me down among the cork tree bushes and tonsured my head. That done, I was made to dip three times in our agricultural tank. When I climbed out of the tank, my uncle handed me the dhoti and told me how to wear it in the traditional fashion. Until that time, I had worn the lower garment only in a horizontal fashion; I needed my uncle's instruction to

* Dasadina karma observed on the tenth day after death.

set me straight. Then, I was made to sit on a low wooden seat near my father's grave. The Brahmin sat on another low seat opposite me. He began to recite some verses in a voice that was both sonorous and monotonous. About twenty feet away from where I sat water flowed in the riverbed. My mother was seated on the sand by the stream; she was being readied for the ritual removal of the turmeric and vermilion spot. The Brahmin made three rings out of sacred grass and slipped them on the three fingers of my right hand. Then he made eight balls of cooked rice and placed them on a banana leaf, all the while chanting verses from the scriptures. Now he paused and in that same sonorous and monotonous voice instructed me to throw a rice ball in each of the eight directions. As I threw the rice balls he resumed his recitation. Then he put some sesame seeds in my palm and poured water from a bronze jug over them so that the sesame seeds were washed into a sacred vase underneath, whose mouth was lined with mango leaves. I carried out all these rituals, but mechanically, just following the Brahmin's instructions. My eyes and ears were solely on my mother. In the ten days since my father's death, her eyes never ceased to be wet and nothing had passed her lips. Within this short time, she had become half her size, and now she was seated on the sand near the streambed, pining and silent.

I saw my uncle hurriedly walking over the sand towards the crowd of women. He went up to my aunt and seemed to give her some instructions while at the same time pointing to the sun. Whereupon, my aunt rose up tucking her sari-end around her waist, removed the glass bangles from my mother's wrists, and smashed them on a stone. She took the silver rings off my mother's toes and the gold jewels from her nose and ears and placed them on a towel spread on the sand. Then ever so respectfully, she removed the sacred marriage cord with the thali* on it from my mother's neck. She tucked the cord into her own waistband, for tradition dictates that under no circumstances should a sacred marriage cord touch the ground. Then she pulled the flowers from my mother's braid and threw them in the stream. I can still see the yellow marigolds and the white jasmine flowers floating down the stream, bobbing on the ripples.

To that point, though still silently grieving, my mother had cooperated docilely with every move my aunt made. But when she attempted to erase the red spot** on my mother's forehead, Amma resisted. She

* Thali, the symbol of marriage.
** Vermilion (bottu) on the forehead is the symbol of a woman's married status, which she is permitted to retain for only ten days after her husband's death.

covered her forehead with her hands and resisted with all her strength. Another woman from the crowd was called in to help. She grasped my mother's arms and pulled, trying to break her grip on her forehead. Amma held out against them for quite some time, clenching her teeth, thrashing her legs in the sand, and not giving into them. But in the end, they pulled her hands away. My aunt quickly rubbed off the red spot and then washed her own hands in the stream. Now my mother sat bolt upright, looking about her wildly and as if possessed, and then let out a terrifying scream that subsided to moaning and wailing. And she began beating her breasts. Even as the women watched helplessly, she wailed and moaned, crushing the dry leaves where she rolled in the sand. A water bird that had been racking up the sand for worms stopped its search and craned about bewildered. Then it flew up clumsily and landed on the other side of the stream quacking furiously, fading further and further into a bamboo grove, never once stopping its mad quacking.

The Brahmin despite himself, left off chanting the verses and turned his head to look. I half rose from my wooden seat, but he put his hands on my shoulders and pushed me down, while resuming his recitation. In his perplexity, he recited faster and faster until the verses just tumbled out. But I heard almost nothing. I was numb with my Amma's grief.

Condemned

Bakkireddy lay back on his cot. The moaning and wailing in the courtyard had long since died down. His heart had stopped pounding against his chest and was beating normally. The sun had cooled considerably. The shadow cast by the cattleshed lengthened and stretched across the street. The crows that had been out foraging all day returned to the tamarind tree. Perched on its branches they were making a raucous din. Since midday he had confined himself to his cattleshed.

Where could he go, after all?

Why he could have gone to neighbour Narasimha Naidu, who lived on Temple Street.

He could sit with Narasimha under the hayrick behind his house and talk about the vagaries of the weather. 'It has been sweltering for two days. Looks like we might see the first rains tomorrow or day after tomorrow. The clouds might descend over in the northeast corner. Then again they might come down in the southeast corner. How much rain would we get? May be so little that the plough shear would not cut more than four fingers deep. Or, may be so much that the river would flood and the tanks fill the sluices and spillways.' Issues such as these he would talk over with his neighbours. 'But I am no longer a farmer', he thought, 'I have lost my land. What would it matter to me if the tank was full or dry? For that matter, why should I care even if thorn trees grew in the tank?'

But where could he go, after all?

He could go to Gangireddy, who lived on Lower Street. He could sit with him on the pyol and talk about crops, 'Which of the varieties of paddy suits this season? How high would such and such paddy grow? Which pest would give the paddy most trouble? How many months would it take for whatever paddy to grow through milk seed? And how many weeks would it take to harden and be ready for harvesting? And what would be the per acre yield?' Matters such as these he could discuss with his friend. 'But I am no longer a farmer myself' he said to himself, 'my land has been snatched from me, the way a chick was snatched from a mother's hen by a hawk. As things now stand, I am not even worthy of sitting next to Gangireddy.'

Where could he go, after all?

Why, he could go to the carpenter who lived on Boulder Street. There was a shack behind the carpenter's house, which was his workshop. There he was always seen, busy with saws, chisels, adzes, draw knives, and planes, all the usual tools of the trade. He could go to him and say, 'Friend, I must have a new plough ready before the day is over. Look at the way the clouds are moving! The first rains are sure to begin in a day or two. The Brahmin consulted the almanac and pronounced as much. The minute the rain drops touch the ground, I must harness the plough and before the moisture is sucked up I must plough my field at least three times. Problems such as these he could share with the carpenter. But I am no longer a farmer,' he reminded himself, 'I sold my land in an auction like King Harischandra* sold his wife. What need do I have for a new plough? What would it matter to me, even if the old one was eaten by termites?'

Where would he go, after all?

Why, he could go to the blacksmith, who also lived in Boulder Street. His smithy was under a tamarind tree not far from his house. There he could always be seen banging away on his anvil working with his hammer and tongs on some piece of iron. Bakkireddy could say to him, 'Friend, you must spare some time for me. For my bulls need your service urgently. Their hooves are worn away and blood is dripping from them. They need to be new shod at once. Can you come to my house with your implements or do you want me to bring the bulls here?' Favours such as these he could seek for him. 'But

* King Harischandra, paupered by the power of Saturn, was forced to auction his wife.

I am not a farmer any longer' he mused, 'I've lost my land the way a mother loses her child in an abortion. It could make no difference whether the bulls are in the cattleshed or killed and devoured by leopards.'

Suddenly, the bat stirred in the wall niche and fluttered clumsily into the air. It flew round and round in the shed and then up into the loft where it was swallowed up in the darkness. Bakkireddy kept staring into the darkness.

So then, that was his lot. He had lost his land. All the connections that had joined him to the earth were broken. Now he had nothing to do with anyone in the village. He could never show his face again anywhere. There was nothing left for him to do on this earth of animates and inanimates. He was condemned to a life of darkness, like the bat that lived in the loft or an owl that lives in the hollow of a tree. Now, for all intents and purposes, he was nothing but deadwood on earth. From now on the men and women of the village would fear him and avoid him, for the very sight of him would be taken for an evil omen. Should a group of villagers that had set out on a hopeful errand run into him they would stop their journey on the spot and return home, just as if a black cat had crossed their path. The men and women of the village would stigmatize him and loathe his very name: the very synonym for ill luck. And for generation after generation the people of the village would not give his name or anything that sounded like it to their children. Bakkireddy rolled over on his cot and lay on his side. The bulls rose to their feet near their tethering stakes. The evening was coming on and the tormenting gadflies were already busy. The bulls kept swishing their tails, trying to drive them away. As it grew darker, the crows in the tamarind tree increased their racket. Thousands and thousands of fireflies glimmered in the leaves and branches.

The Bull

After some time, Bakkireddy heard the voices of men talking in the street. The voices became clearer and more distinct; he knew they were coming in his direction. He sat up on his cot and saw a kerosene lantern moving at the same height as three pairs of legs. Presently, three men came into the cattleshed. They were his fellow farmers: Raypati Gangireddy, Galla Narsihma Naidu, and Pakala Munireddy. The three of them came up to the cot. Gangireddy put the lantern down by the stone pillar and seated himself on the cot. The other two sat down on a log near the cot. The four men had been companions since childhood.

In the days of their youth they used to play their four-square game in the streets and swim in the agricultural tank to the north of the village. In the summer season when the Kangudi* drama troupe arrived in the village to enact their plays, the four friends would sneak into the audience, unnoticed by their elders, and watch the shows. And as for the puppet theatre, the four never missed a performance and were in their seats long before the prologue came on stage to begin the show. When they were old enough, one after another they were married. At each wedding, one of them served as best man to the groom. And after the wedding, each one conducted himself as brother or brother-in-law to the other's wife. When the children came, each of the friends became maternal and paternal uncles to the children born to the others.

The four friends helped each other in their farming, sharing tools, and implements. During the harvest season they took turns watching over the ripened crops at night. Thus, in all their years in the village not a day passed without meeting at least once. 'But that story was true only until yesterday, not any longer,'

---

* Performing mythological street plays in the summer months is the traditional occupation of a few families in Kangundi village (Chittoor district).

Bakkireddy said to himself. 'Today I am a nomad, a vagabond, a beggar without land. These men are farmers, as good as lords. In fact they've come here to make fun of me, to take a dig at me. Each of them, I'm sure, has brought along two cups, one filled with charcoal powder and the other with white lime paste. If I even dare to lift my eyes and look at them, they will grab me and smear my face with the charcoal and dab white spots all over it.'

He sat on the cot, silently dangling his legs, his face distraught, his eyes cast down, like Yudhishtira* when Draupadi questioned his authority to stake her in the game of dice, or when Arjuna questioned his wisdom in sending Abhimanyu alone into the chakravyuh battle formation. But his friends did not question him, nor comment on his condition. They just sat there, looking at him, saying nothing, waiting for something to happen to break the ice. Then the two bulls that were standing at their tethers started to swing their heads and stamp the ground restlessly. Narsihma Naidu lifted

---

* Yudhishtira staked his wife Draupadi in the game of dice without so much as informing her and when he lost the game his enemies claimed her as their slave. Yudhishtira persuaded Abhimanyu, the valiant but young son of Arjuna to penetrate a very unique battle formation (chakravyuh), planned and executed by the Kauravas to isolate and kill him.

the lantern and looked at the bulls. 'Why are they so restless, friend? I don't think you have watered them once since morning, have you?' Gangireddy put in 'Why do you ask our friend? You can see for yourself how their flanks are sunken in. Do take them out and water them yourself.' Narsihma got up from the log, untethered the bulls, and took them to the water trough. After they drank to their hearts' content, he brought them back and tied them to their stakes again. Sitting back down on the log he said, 'They drank a whole trough-full of water! In one draught! Didn't leave a drop! You can guess how thirsty they were.' He turned to Bakkireddy and asked reproachfully, 'What is this, my friend? Why have you neglected them so? Is it becoming of a farmer?' Bakkireddy looked at him sharply and shouted, 'I am not a farmer now. I have not got an inch of land to my name. Why do you call me a farmer?'

All three of the friends were a little taken back. And Gangireddy said, 'When did you start talking this kind of nonsense, friend? You were born a farmer, and what are you if not a farmer?' Bakkireddy quickly ran his eyes over the faces of his friends, back and forth. His eyes danced wildly in the light of the lantern. 'My birth! Who knows anything at all what my birth was. What proof do I have now to be able to claim I'm a farmer? I lost my land. I lost an expanse of five acres and washed my hands. Now I'm a vagabond, a nomad, a street beggar. Yes, I'm a street beggar. And you have all come here to remind me of precisely that. You're here to ridicule and rag me.'

'Now, now' Gangireddy replied, raising his hand in protest, 'such self-condemnation is uncalled for, friend. Everything comes to pass in fulfilment of what is written on the forehead. True, the land is lost. But that is not the end of the world. You had better try to see what can be seen now, rather than indulging in self-blame and pity.' 'What is there to be seen?' asked Bakkireddy in a much softer voice. 'I am orphaned by my land. Surely, you can't expect me to survive this loss. As things stand, friend, I have only two options – to hang myself or drink pesticide. I will do one or the other, and very soon. I no longer have a right to exist on earth.' His friends fell silent and said nothing for the time being. Gangireddy looked at Narasimha Naidu and Narasimha Naidu looked at Munireddy. In the light of the lantern, three pairs of eyes held a conference. Without saying a word, the three of them came to understand that something had to be done and nodded in agreement. Gangireddy got to his feet and put his hand on Bakkireddy's shoulder. 'I presume you haven't had a thing to eat since morning, have you?' Bakkireddy answered in a voice so feeble it might have come from the bottom of a well sixty feet deep. 'How can I eat, friend? The land was everything to me. I lost it. How can food go down my throat? How can these eyes ever find sleep?'

'I thought as much. Now, may I suggest then that you get up and go out with us?'

'Where to?'

'I'll tell you in a minute, but please do get up.' Gangireddy held him by the arms and lifted him up. Bakkireddy stood there asking, 'Where? Where do you want us to go?'

'Not far. Just four steps – not a step more than four – to the toddy shop.'

'The toddy shop? What business do I have there?'

'Listen, friend, we're farmers, too, and we know what it's like to lose land. We do. At the moment your heart must ache like a raw wound. The aching won't stop until you get two bottles into your stomach.'

Bakkireddy stiffened immediately and pushed his friend away. His face reddened and his lips began to tremble. 'What? You want me to drink toddy! What do you take me for?' he growled at his friends. 'Today you want me to drink toddy. Tomorrow you'll want me to walk the streets with a begging bowl in my hands. And the day after tomorrow you will want me to sit on the steps of the Tirupathi Hills!'* I know this game. You want to make fun of me. You've come here to revel at my expense. That's why you're here!'

The friends were stunned by this outburst and had no reply. It took some time, and not a short time, for them to regain their wits. They were just about to speak their protest when one of the bulls – the white one – bellowed loudly. Bakkireddy turned right away and stared at it. The bull was standing majestically at its tethering stake. It tossed its head sending out a challenging call, waiting for an opponent to answer. As they all watched, the bull bellowed defiantly for a second and third time, pawing up the ground with his right fore-hoof. Small clods of earth were thrown high into the air and fell back on its head and shoulders.

'Did you see that? Did you see the insolence?' roared Bakkireddy. 'Even the bull makes fun of me. This accursed animal which ate at my farm and drank from my trough – even he looks down on me. Every wretched creature thinks it can look down on me now because I have no land.' He looked around and found a club leaning against a wall. It was about as thick as his

* The holy shrine of Lord Venkateswara is situated on Tirupathi hills; beggars squat on the steps leading to the shrine and pester pilgrims for alms.

arm and five or six feet long. He picked the club up in both hands, lifted it over his head, and brought it down on the bull's flank. The animal was startled; it turned its head and looked in bewilderment at its master. A second blow came crashing down on its nose. Relentlessly, brutally the club rose and fell raining down all over its body – on flanks, back, legs, hump, and head. The shed reverberated with the thudding of the club. The bull writhed and squirmed in pain. When the pain became unbearable the animal put out its tongue and began to low pathetically. The lowing mingled with the thudding of the club filling the shed with agonizing sounds. But Bakkireddy could no longer hear the pathetic lowing of the bull. The sounds of the first defiant bellowing shrilled in his ear and deafened him. Nor could he see the animal writhing in pain; all the defiant pawing up of the ground had made him blind with rage. Thus both blind and deaf to the animal's agony, he went on bashing and hammering, as if to make a mincemeat of it. Sweat poured down his face and he panted with fatigue.

His friends tried to restrain him, but he pushed them aside. 'Away! Away from me! Either I must die today or this ill-born creature must. As for me, I will die in a day or two anyway. But this creature! He was brought up under my care. I fed him with my own grain. And today he makes fun of me. I will kill him and bury him before

I die!' And though panting and swaying from fatigue, he kept up his savage attack. The bull no longer writhed or lowed. Instead, it backed and backed to the full length of its tether rope. It braced itself and tugged at the rope with all its strength. Every part of its body strained to be free, from the twirling tail to its foam-drenched tongue and bulging eyes. But the rope did not break; it was made of aloe fibres and was very strong.

The friends could no longer bear to watch the torturing of the animal and Narsihma Naidu slid along the wall of the shed, skirted around the stone pillar, and was able to undo the knot at the stake. In an instant, the bull leaped back and landed outside the shed. Another leap and it landed in the street, then whirled round and galloped off headlong into the village. As it ran, its iron-shod hooves struck flashes of sparks. Never once looking back or slowing its wild pace, as if it were still being bashed with the club wielded by an unseen hand, the bull ran and ran through all the streets of the village until it passed a toddy shop in the outskirts and slowed to a trot. When it reached the canal it stopped and dropped its head to the water and drank and drank. Many of the villagers saw with their own eyes the white bull running through the streets; many more heard with their own ears the heavy pounding of its hooves. And they asked each other what might have caused a bull to run like that.

'Probably the bull was stung by a wasp. You know, that nasty kind with a red underbelly that can drive the strongest bull crazy. Oh yes, they can.'

'Maybe the bull saw a grass snake in the manger. Of course I know the grass snake isn't poisonous. But it looks so frightening it would scare the life out of you.' Yet another man, drunk and lounging in the village square, drawled, 'Must've been drunk. The way he was pounding down the road with his tail way up in the clouds he must've drunk a trough full of toddy instead of water. Yesh, shir, a whole trou … full.'

By the time the second watch of the night had come to a close, all the speculation about the bull's behaviour was put to rest. People were beginning to whisper that Bakkireddy had lost his mind. The loss of his land had driven him mad; everyone began to say, 'Bakkireddy is crazy.' The rumour ran through the streets and alleys as fast as the bull had run through them. By dawn, the air was thick with the rumour.

The Karanam

Bakkireddy has gone mad.

The report reached even the Karanam. He lived in a tiled house that had a long corridor leading away from the main street of the village. A small room at the end of the corridor was his office. It had a table and a few chairs. Standing against the wall was a wooden cupboard that held all the registers and records of the land deeds of every farmer in the village. It was the duty of the Karanam to maintain the registers and update them periodically.

Presently the Karanam entered the office, opened the cupboard, took down one of the large registers, and laid it open on the table. Then he sat down, dipped the pen in the ink pot, and seemed about to write something but put down his pen and with a deep sigh leaned back in his chair tipping it against wall.

'Karanam sir! Are you in?' A voice called from the street.

'Yes, I'm here, I'm here. Please come in.'

A villager entered in and sat in one of the chairs, and wiped the sweat of his brow with his upper cloth.

'What is the matter, brother?' asked the Karanam.

'Ah, since last full-moon day I have been coming around to your office. And, here you are asking, "What is the matter, brother!" Look, sir, I cannot get on with my brother any longer. All the income from the land he spends on women. You must go with me, measure the land and then divide it into two, and tell me which is mine and which is his.'

'Land – land,' said the Karanam tonelessly, 'at the time of our arrival in this world, brother, none of us brings any land and at the time of departure no one takes any away with him, either. Look what's happened to poor Bakkireddy.'

'Oh, yes, I hear that he has gone insane since he lost his land. How did that come about, sir?'

'Well,' said the Karanam, 'He kept raising loans rather recklessly until one day he found himself neck deep in debt. The bank people came down finally and auctioned off his land to recover their money.'

'That is just what I don't understand. One should stretch his legs only as far as his cot permits. Why did he go and borrow money left and right?' 'You can be sure it was not to spend on women, like your brother,' answered the Karanam. 'All the money went into his well. You know how it is. The rains lifted and soon enough the well went dry. He thought if he had the well deepened by two fathoms he'd hit water again. But, brother, even after two fathoms he found no water.'

'I know, sir. If the stars are not in your favour, you will strike neither water nor ashes.'

'He came to me, to me you understand, for help to fill out the loan applications. And I did it with these same accursed hands. But I warned him before I filled out the papers. I told him the bank people are corpse-eaters. I asked him to think about how he was going to pay the amount when the time was up. But he wouldn't take my advice. No, not at all, and said that the well was dry, that cork bushes were growing in the bottom, that termites were getting at his plough, and that his bulls had a large growth of hair on their necks from not being yoked and driven. And then said, "Tell me, Karanam sir, how long can I – a born farmer – sit about with my arms folded?" So he raised a loan of twelve thousand rupees and spent it all on the well.'

'And even after spending so much money, he got no water?'

'Never mind water, brother, it wasn't even damp at the bottom of the well. But I have to say that he was a very strong-willed man. He wanted to deepen the well by another two fathoms. And again it was my lot to help write the application for the new loan. I gave my counsel as best I could. I did. I warned him he was venturing too far. I told him to seriously consider how he would manage the repayment. But he was bursting with confidence. He laughed at me and twirled his moustache, 'Bah! Let me strike water, Karanam sir, then you will know what I am. With the very first crop I will clear half of the loan and with the second crop, I'll clear off the remainder. In two years – just within two years, mind you – I will get back the loan papers and show them to you. If I fail, you shall not call me Bakkireddy…. And so he raised a second loan of twelve thousand rupees and squandered the whole amount in that well. In all he must have deepened that well by some four fathoms. And for all that he managed to strike, as you put it, neither water nor ashes.'

'But why was he so sure he would strike water? What gave him such confidence?'

'It was the tank digger. The tank-digger talked him into it. He stirred hope in the brain of that simpleton.'

'Well, a tank-digger is a professional, too. He may say a thousand things. But where was the man's common sense?'

'It is the power of Saturn, brother', said the Karanam. 'When the power of that evil star is upon you, your common sense takes leave of you. Tell me, why did Yudhishtira* play the game of dice? Was it due to lack of common sense? No, he played because the power of Saturn was upon him. It's as simple as that.' The Karanam sat silently, staring at the land register still open on the table, much as Yudhishtira had sat dejected after losing stake after stake. The villager fidgeted in his chair as if suddenly remembering why he had come there in the first place and said, 'But, Karanam sir, what about my problem now. When will you come and measure the land?'

---

* Yudhishtira, son of Kunti, the eldest Pandava prince, the epitome of righteousness (Mahabharata).

'I see you are in a hurry, brother. But why? There is no need. That land isn't going anywhere. I'll come along and carry out the survey. That's my job, that's what I'm paid for. But hang on for a while, just now the very word "land" makes me sick.... Oh. When I think of what has happened to Bakkireddy, I begin to hate my job. Come back to see me in four or five days.'

'So be it,' the villager said and got up from the chair, throwing the upper-cloth over his shoulder. He left the room muttering to himself, 'Yes, there is a great truth in it. At the time of arriving in this world, no one comes carrying his land with him. And at the time of leaving no one takes it along with him, either. There is great truth in it.'

The Tank-digger

Bakkireddy has gone mad.

The news reached the headman of the tank-diggers' hamlet, which lies on the other side of the main highway not far from the village. About fifteen huts made up the habitation. The tank-diggers' main occupation comprised constructing water tanks and digging wells. But they also made pillars and blocks, out of granite boulders. It was they indeed who dug the wells, tanks, and canals in the province and provided the stone used to build houses, choultries, and temples. And of course, they were the ones who chipped and split the stones to make gravel for the roads. As the day broke the headman rose from his mat outside his hut, then went into it, and came out with a pot of toddy. He sat down on the pyol and put the pot up to his lips. He drained half of it in a single gulp, then put the pot down beside him. Since he spent the whole day under a blazing sun digging in the earth or hewing granite blocks by sundown, every joint and muscle in his body would ache. And to ease the pain, he drank freely in the evening. But this morning it was not to ease his aching body that he drank. At around midnight, the news of Bakkireddy had reached him. From that moment he couldn't sleep. When the first cock crowed from under the wattle basket, when the pole star appeared in the sky, when the first hint of dawn showed in the east, he was still awake on his sleeping mat. And when he rose from the mat at daybreak, his eyes were red and smarting from lack of sleep. He wiped the drops of toddy that clung to his moustache and said to himself, 'The lord of a granary he was until yesterday. And today he is a pauper.... Phoo! Accursed god! Accursed god!' He picked up the toddy pot again and emptied it in one swallow. His wife who had been rinsing their earthenware bowls in the backyard stopped her work and looked askance at him, then went on with her work. The headman stepped down from the pyol and wound his upper cloth around his head. When he looked up he noticed a farmer coming round the bend in the street and approaching him. When the farmer drew near enough, he called out politely, 'Ah, sir, is that you? Surprised that you would actually come to our village so early in the morning.'

'I've come to see you, friend, for I have need of your service. I came early because I know that once the sun is up you will not be available.' 'What service is it that you want from me, sir?' He moved the toddy pot off the pyol. 'Please, sit down, if you like.'

'It's this well of mine, friend, may the plague take it.' The farmer sat down on the pyol and said, 'It's gone completely dry; there's not a half cup of water in it, not a palmful. It has to be deepened by a fathom or two.' Instead of answering him, the headman lifted his head and scanned the sky from one end to the other.

'What are you rolling your eyes for, friend?' asked the farmer.

'Look at those clouds, sir,' said the headman, pointing to the sky, 'They are moving about like never before.

This month, June, too, is almost over. It looks like we will have rain for sure this year. And once it rains the wells will fill up again. So I am thinking, wouldn't it be wiser for you to hold on till then?'

The farmer looked up at the clouds contemptuously and said, 'Those clouds? They would double-cross their own mothers. Clouds have been taunting us farmers for three years – three very long years.' Then he looked directly into the headman's eyes and said, 'By the way, what is this, friend? Here I am offering you work and you are turning it down. What do you mean by that? If the work isn't to your liking, just tell me. I'll go to another tank-digger.'

'No, sir, it is not that. What is a tank-digger born for if not to dig wells? The point I was trying to make is that one cannot be certain of striking water even after deepening a well by a fathom or two. Think of what happened to Bakkireddy. Just think sir!

At the very mention of Bakkireddy, the farmer fell silent and remained so for a long time, still sitting on the pyol. Then he sighed deeply and threw up his hands towards the sky. 'It is His will. But I, too, must do my bit, or how will four fingers slip into my mouth. Without water in the well, without being able to till the land, how long can I just sit on my backside flapping my ears?'

'Sir, that is just the way Bakkireddy spoke,' said the headman sighing sadly. '"Water, I must strike water! I'll go to any length to raise the money. But there's no question of going back on that score." That was what he said, Bakkireddy, the poor simpleton, so we went on digging. At the end of the first two fathoms, I came upon fish-scale boulders and that in itself was a bad enough sign. After going down another two fathoms, what did I see? Nothing, but red-streaked boulders. Now I can tell you from long experience, once you meet red-streaked boulders you might as well abandon the well. No matter how many fathoms deeper you might go from there, you will not find water. And I told Bakkireddy as much. But the good man would not believe me. He would not. So he fetched a tank-digger from a far off village. Now this stranger was a famous soil appraiser. He went down the well and spent a great deal of time examining the properties of the boulders and soil at the bottom. After completing his inspection, he climbed back up the well and told Bakkireddy exactly what I had already told him. That was all, sir. The man went to pieces. Veritable tiger that he was, he was suddenly a little boy. And like a little boy he began to weep. Even as we watched, the tears welled and ran down his cheeks, then he slumped to the ground like a banana tree felled at its base. "Is that all my life is to be, friend? Is that all? Am I not destined to die like a farmer? In which future births will I be destined to hold the plough handle? Oh, when I think of that, sir," the headman went on, "my bowels flame and begin to roast."'

'Is that why you have drunk a whole pot of toddy first thing this morning?' the farmer asked, peering into the empty toddy pot. Getting no answer, he was silent for a while as though pondering over some deep question. At last he shook his head and said, 'Why must you bring up all that and make yourself delirious, my friend? What is certain on this earth? Nothing. Everything is unstable. The rains are undependable. The wells are undependable. The crops are undependable – our very lives are so fickle. But even so, even in the face of all this uncertainty and instability we must go on with our duties. After all, we can't be like that proverbial woman who refused to light the kitchen fire because she feared some visitor might come along wanting to be fed, can we?' He jumped off the stone bench. 'Now, about that well of mine. Tell me when are you going to start working on it?'

The question did not register with the headman. He just stood there with his head bowed, weighing the farmer's words. Then he looked up and said, 'It is true, sir, in spite of fickleness and uncertainty we must carry on with our tasks. A man who shuns such duties is no better than those lifeless boulders that lie strewn there on the mountain slope.'

'That's it. So tell me, when will you begin work on my well?'

'It's for you to name the day, sir, and I will begin the work that very day.'

'What is there to name? You know where the well is; you have the shovels and picks. It's for you to say what day suits you.'

'Well, then, tomorrow is Friday and the lunar day of the month,' said the headman, counting the days on his fingers, 'and the day after tomorrow is the second lunar day. Let these two days pass. On Sunday I will come along with my men and begin work.'

'Agreed,' said the farmer, 'I'll be waiting for you on Sunday morning.' He took his upper cloth, placed it over his shoulder and walked towards the street, muttering, 'No doubt, he has contracted Bakkireddy fever. No question of it. Seems the whole village is going to be in the grip of the fever soon. The whole village.'

Maniam

Bakkireddy has gone mad.

The news reached the Maniam. By the time the sun had risen four fathoms high in the sky, the Maniam was in his office at the Village Council as was his usual custom. The corridor was littered with dry leaves and bits of paper. Normally the Thalari would have reached an hour or so earlier and cleaned up the offices and corridor and you would find him seated on the steps of the building waiting for the Administrator. The people who came to seek the Maniam's advice and counsel sat on the benches in the corridor leaning against the wall. Today, however, the corridor looked deserted. The Maniam had to unlock the door of his office himself. He entered and sat down at his desk. He looked around the room, taking in the walls, windows, and the ceiling and felt as if he had been flung into a dungeon, even into the deepest part of hell. In a short while, the Thalari came along holding his quarter-staff in one hand and his coarse sandals in the other. He stood in the corridor and said, 'I salute you, Master.' The Administrator did not pull him up for being late. On the contrary, he asked, 'What brings you here, friend?'

Taken aback by the odd, irrelevant question, he replied, 'It ... it is the collection of the tax, Master. The work is not yet completed.'

'What tax, friend?' asked the Maniam despondently.

'The land tax, Master. You had said the collection of the land tax had to be completed by the lunar day and tomorrow is the lunar day.'

'Yes, tomorrow is the lunar day, and the Tahasildar*
will be here the day after tomorrow.' He paused and
asked, 'How many farmers have yet to pay their tax?'

'Six of them, master, if you omit Bakkireddy. I can
complete the work by sundown today.'

'I heard that Bakkireddy has lost his mind,' said the
Administrator not without some hesitation in his voice,
'do you know anything about that?'

'Yes, Master, I heard so first thing this morning.
Immediately, I went to see him. He is lying in the cattle
shed, just staring vacantly at anyone who comes to see
him hardly opening his mouth. And when he speaks, his
talk is incoherent. He is completely unhinged, Master.'
He turned up his palms in a gesture of despair and
added, 'To imagine a farmer so obsessed with his land
that the moment he loses it, he is robbed of his reason!
True, I never owned even a palm-width of land myself.
Nonetheless, I can't get over what I felt when I saw him
lying on his back in his cattleshed.'

The Maniam was about to say something but
restrained himself. He fell silent, head bowed, thinking.
In this very office many farmers had lost their lands
in auction. He knew them all by name. Some of them

* Tahasildar is a revenue official who collects land tax from
the Maniam and remits it to the district treasury.

went on to work for daily wages. Some of them became sharecroppers. Still others left the village and emigrated to far off lands. But there were some who felt their lives had come to nothing the minute their lands were gone. Bakkireddy was one such. History tells of many kings who lost their realms. Some of them went on to live as commoners. Some others lived in asylum in another kingdom. Still others lived as captives of their conquerors. And there were also some who felt their lives had come to naught the moment their kingdoms were lost.

One such king was Mogili Kolandareddy, an ancestor of the Maniam.

Mogili Kolandareddy had been chieftain of this province in the bygone days. When the British* set about subduing these local chieftains one by one, Kolandareddy began a fierce war of resistance and held out against them for four long years. In the end a large detachment of soldiers with powerful weapons came down from Chennapatnam. Faced with the overwhelming power of those weapons, the chieftain's army had no chance and collapsed. The chieftain with a handful of his aides and

* Thomas Munroo, Principle Collector of Ceded Districts liquidated about 60 Polygars (local chieftains) during the period between 1801–1807. Most of them were killed, some taken captive, and a few took their own lives.

allies fled the fort and took shelter in a cave near the top of a mountain not far from the village. The British managed to learn of his whereabouts and cordoned off the hill. A messenger was dispatched to the chieftain with a warning that it would be best for him to surrender without further resistance; then the supplies of food and water were cut off. Eight days passed. Unable to bear their hunger and thirst, his men came down the hill one after the other and surrendered. Kolandareddy was alone on the hill top. Still, the soldiers did not dare to climb up the hill. On the ninth day, they noticed a few vultures circling over the highest point of the hill. The soldiers with their guns ready, moved up the hill from all sides, by midday they made it to the top. They found Kolandareddy lying in a pool of blood in front of the cave, his dagger in his chest.

The Maniam sat with his head bowed, still engrossed in his reminiscence. The thalari took a step forward and said, 'Master, do you bid me to go about collecting the taxes?' But the Maniam looked up and said unenthusiastically, 'No, friend, not today. Some other day. As for the Tahasildar, I will see him as and when he comes.' He lowered his eyes and added, 'Now, if you have any personal business to attend to, please go about it.' The servant looked perplexed, but turned and slowly climbed down the steps.

The Clouds

Clouds began to fill half the sky, clouds of different colours, some black, other white, yet other saffron and they were of various shapes, now banyan trees, then elephants, and still other like giant humans. The very earth of animate and inanimate things seemed to be reflected in the sky. We know that life here on earth is unreal and that there seems to be nothing in it but constant change. So, one could expect that its reflection in the sky would only be more unreal and the changes even faster. Thus, the cloud that was black a while ago now acquired a saffron colour. And the cloud that was white is now black. The cloud that looked like a banyan tree now looks like an elephant. And the cloud that looked like an elephant now resembles a huge human head.

So, changing their shapes and colours the clouds moved on slowly to the northeast. Bakkireddy laid on his cot curled up like a foetus in its mother's womb. His chest rose and fell gently. His eyes were closed, but the eyeballs flickered beneath the lids. Since yesterday, all manner of people had been calling on him in the cattle shed: his wife, relatives, fellow farmers, local artisans, and many more. They were friends, relatives, and well-wishers only until yesterday. But as things stood now, the whole world had become distant and alien. He no longer responded to the sounds his bulls made in the cattle shed or to the cawing of the crows in the tamarind tree. He no longer had any sense of having any connection with people or birds or animals. There was the earth, true enough, but he no longer felt linked to it or with its millions of creatures.

Perhaps the bat might be the only creature with which he could possibly relate. The bat, his bat, lay cuddled in a corner of the loft. At sunset, it would emerge from the loft. It would fly over the village, over the pastures, the graves, rivers, valleys, and grain fields as it wished. It would meet its friends and in its squeaky language converse, quarrel, and compromise with them. In their company it would hunt mice, squirrels, and grasshoppers and make a feast from the spoils of the hunt. Having spent the night in merriment and gaiety, it would set about on its return journey home. And long before daybreak, it would be back in the loft. They claim that the bat is a creature given to darkness and devilry. The claim isn't altogether valid when one thinks of the intense and boundless zeal with which it pursues its life. But to see any parallel between the lives of Bakkireddy and the bat would be preposterous and absurd.

Truly, no one ever lived so futile and despised an existence as he had. And no one would in the future.

It made no difference whether he lay on a cot, a foot, or so above ground or in a grave knee-deep beneath it. Now that he had lost the land and any zeal to go on living, he was as good as dead. There was nothing to look forward to. And he felt he might as well be dead. And when dead, he was certain that a star would fall from the sky. For he had heard it said that there were as many stars in the sky as there were people living on the earth. And that each man on earth was represented by a star. So when a man died the star that represented him would fall as a shooting star. So what then of his own star? Probably it was poised to shoot down. Probably it would streak across the sky at any moment now.

And after death?

What?

His knowledge of the after-life was, alas, meagre. The Brahmin used to touch upon such issues when expounding the scriptures on the occasions of festivals and holy days. But Bakkireddy never paid much attention to what he said. He took it for granted that such matters were all but exclusively the business of the Brahmin. And anyway he never felt he had the faculties to consider the subtleties of the issue. After death, out there in the other world, there were certain things he was duty bound to look forward to. Most important would be the encounter with his father. And his father would inquire about many things. Above all, he would ask about the land.

Suddenly, Bakkireddy opened his eyes. As if he had been lashed with a whip, he quickly rose and sat bolt upright on the cot. Someone seemed to have been calling him for a long time, 'Bakka, O Bakka, what have you done with the land, son?'

Whose voice was that? His father's. Indeed the voice was his father's! He leapt off the cot and ran out of the cattleshed and then behind his house, but there was no one to be seen. Still the voice called him again and again, now in a low tone and again at a high pitch. He looked up and there in the sky he saw a gigantic image of his father's face. His turban was all saffron, his bushy moustache stained brown from the chewing tobacco always in his mouth. He stared down and asked, 'The land, Bakka, what has become of the land, son?'

He was faint from having jumped up so suddenly after lying down for so long; his eyes went dark and he fell down sideways like a stack of firewood. The bulls in the cattleshed were startled and rose to their feet. And up there in the sky the huge human head-shaped cloud slowly dissolved and turned into a banyan tree, while the thunder still roared and cracked, up and down the scale.

The Sun

When he came to, Bakkireddy found himself lying on the cot. A large pillow had been put behind his head. His wife had applied some liquid on his palms and the soles of his feet and was rubbing them. Then she brought him a full glass of milk and held it to his lips so that he could drink it in sips. After he finished the whole glass, he opened his eyes, which forced a faint smile from her. She tried to converse with him, speaking softly and gesturing with her hands. But his ears heard no sound, his eyes see no gesture. He saw nothing but his father's face that filled the whole of space and heard nothing but his voice resounding through heaven and earth. It was the land that his father had spoken of as he lay on his death bed. 'Land, land – he must keep the land. I will be gone in a day or two, but my soul will always be upon the land. And my son – he cannot tell east from west. He is only a child.' Those indeed were his words as he breathed his last. At the time, Bakkireddy had an answer for his father's doubts. Looking straight into his eyes and pushing his chest forward, he said, 'I will keep the land, father. Of course I will. I will protect the land like the eyelid protects the eye. For I was born to a farmer, not to a vagabond.'

But he did not keep his word. He had failed miserably, failed in every sense of the word, and his failure was catastrophic. With this sense of failure weighing down upon him, how could he face his father and answer his question? Who could help him in this dilemma? Who would be the arbitrator between him and his father? He desperately called to mind all his acquaintances, fellow farmers, artisans, shop keepers, the priest, the school master, and many others. But none was able to help him; they all belonged to the terrestrial world. How could any one of them possibly play the arbitrator in an issue that lay between him and his father – who was in the celestial world? Perhaps one of the gods might be able to offer a solution to his problem. But which god? He had heard the Brahmin say that the gods were as many as three crore in number and that the sun was one of them. Now, his familiarity and close acquaintance with the sun god could not be over-emphasized. For was it not true that he spent the long hours of his day working in the heat of the sun, and at night resting in the cooling rays of the sun's brother, the moon? That being so, wouldn't the sun god help him with a solution? Would he not be willing to play the arbitrator between him and his father?

Those were the thoughts that rambled in his mind, drifting here and there aimless, and irrelevant like the prattle of a man drunk or delirious. His eyes, however, were stock still, as though entranced, staring fixedly into the darkness of the niche in the wall.

The red disc of the sun rose up from behind the mountain to the east. It cast its warm level rays on Bakkireddy and seemed to tap him awake. He shifted and sat up on the cot. Above the crest of the mountain, the sun stood red and perfect in its roundness. Sitting on the cot he gazed at the sun and his gaze was unswerving. He observed that the disc of the sun was inching up the sky and slowly, bit by bit, its redness was giving way to white. Then he noticed a black object that had seemed to spring out of the disc; it changed shape constantly as it tottered at the lower rim of the disc. He narrowed his eyes to a slit, squinting at the object, while his forehead wrinkled and creased with concentration. Lo! The black object that had sprung out of the sun was growing larger and larger; what was more, it was coming in his direction. He straightened his back in readiness. In a moment or two, he could perceive that the object was a horse. The black horse trotted up the street and pulled up in front of the cattleshed. The Maniam dismounted and walked into the shed. 'Is that you, brother?' cried out Bakkireddy. 'I knew you would come. I know why you have come and who sent you.'

'What in heaven's name are you talking about, friend?' said the Maniam. 'No one sent me here. I came of my own accord. I've heard that you haven't been yourself since yesterday.'

But Bakkireddy's words bumped into his. 'Come, come, sir; I know everything. God has sent you as His emissary. He asked you to speak to me, and I have a great deal to say to you. Come brother and sit down here beside me.' He caught the Maniam's arm and pulled him down on the cot. The day before the Maniam had heard that Bakkireddy had gone out of his mind. Now he could see it for himself, he looked at him as if he were looking at a little child. And like a little child Bakkireddy babbled animatedly. 'I ask of you a favour and you must oblige. I know you will oblige, because that's the very purpose for your coming here. Shall I ask, brother?'

'Go ahead, friend, whatever it is, ask.'

'You know what I am going to ask. And yet you act as if you didn't know. Well, never mind. Here it is.' Bakkireddy sat cross-legged on the cot. 'Roadside Land is now yours. Five acres of land. Every inch of it is now yours. In that land, brother, under the peepal tree, a little piece of it – only about two fathoms in length and about as much in breadth – you must leave out for me.'

'What for? What will you do with that small piece of land?'

'You know what, but you still ask. So, I shall explain. Here it comes,' Bakkireddy paused for a second, 'in a day or two my soul will abandon my body. Now that I have lost my land, there is no reason for me to be around.

After I'm gone, brother, it is my wish that my mortal remains be buried in that land under the peepal tree. You must see to it that this wish of mine is carried out under your own supervision. Give me your word, give me your word, brother, that you will do it.'

'That's not much to ask. Had you wanted, I would leave out as much as an acre. But you must stop the babbling. Do stop it. Try to get a hold of yourself.'

'Enough, brother. That will do. You've given me your word. That's enough for me. Indeed, brother, you have poured sugar in my mouth and milk in my stomach. Now I don't have to fear my father. Why, I could even ridicule him myself.' Bakkireddy lapsed into silence for a brief moment, then continued, 'You see, brother, when my father was on his death bed, I gave him my word that I would protect the land like the eyelid protects the eye. The minute my father meets me tomorrow, he will ask, "What have you done with the land, Bakka?" Then I'll be able to answer, looking straight into his eyes, "You can see for yourself, father, I am lying right in it, protecting it just as the eyelid protects the eye. See for yourself!" That's what I shall say to him. And now I don't have to fear my father at all....'

The Administrator listened to him attentively, yet every word he spoke seemed to be in a foreign language. He remained seated on the cot, staring silently at the ground, at a loss as what to say in return. He found himself in a situation that was very strange, baffling, and certainly outside any experience of his. But Bakkireddy prompted him, saying, 'Now, brother, I must not hold up you any longer. The sun is now well up and no doubt there are a hundred officers requiring your attention as Maniam.' Then he lay back on the cot, stretched full length, and closed his eyes.

The disc of the sun was no longer red but a dazzling white. As inch by inch it crept up in the sky, so the dark shadows of the eaves of the cattleshed crept down inch by inch and covered his head, his neck, chest, stomach, thighs, legs, feet, and up to his toes.

The Rain

The sky now began to be covered over in heavy clouds from one end of the horizon to the other and soon, try as one might, one could not find a palm width of blue sky. Each cloud differed from the other in colour and size. They were no longer moving to the northeast. Instead they stood where they did, solemn and impregnable. The sun's rays could not penetrate them and the light that filtered down through them was insubstantial, its colour now misty white. The village dogs criss-crossed the streets and barked madly at the light which was hazy, illusory, and strange. The cattle grazing in the pastures lifted their heads skywards and twitched their noses. Some of the steers gored the earth with their horns and bellowed. Red-footed cranes flew back and forth in the sky, disoriented, no longer knowing in which direction their nests lay. The crows in the trees kept up their unholy din, constantly changing their perches, never sure they were on the right tree. Lizards ran up the trees tails first. The hens stalked about as if they were guilty of something and crept into their coop and tucked their heads under their wings.

The wind dropped and the leaves lay flat against their branches. The still air soaked up the humidity and when the humidity reached a threshold the cicadae began their drumming racket. The earth was simmering like cauldron of a washerman, like the kiln of a potter. The villagers removed as many clothes as they decently could, for the humidity was oppressive.

One farmer called out to others, pointing towards the sky, 'Look, look. How the clouds have gathered!'

His neighbour looked up, 'Yes. They are descending in the northeast.'

'So they are. But, look and see. They are descending on all sides and all at once!' howled another farmer beside himself with joy.

'The rains are sure to begin by evening or much earlier,' said another man.

'And it won't be any ordinary sort of rain. Never a bit. A real downpour. A deluge!' said yet another man; his eyes rolling.

'And the river will flood and overflow its banks,' screamed one youth and broke into a song.

'And the tanks! The tanks will fill up and sluices and spill-ways will race with water,' thundered another youth dancing to the rhythm of the song. They quickly abandoned their fields and hurried down the paths to the village carrying all their farming implements on their heads and shoulders. The shepherds, goatherds, and cattle drovers rounded up their animals and moved them into the confines of the village. The laundrymen gathered the clothes they had spread out to dry into bundles, piled the bundles on their donkeys, and set off for home. A good number of the villagers climbed on to the roofs of their houses to repair the thatching with slough grass and palm fronds. The good wives brought in their firewood from the backyards. The whole village was astir with preparations for the impending rains.

The clouds no longer floated in distinct and solitary shapes; they had all melted into one massive cloud that was so big it covered the entire sky, horizon to horizon. Darkness came upon the earth. And the cloud thundered as if announcing the arrival of all the angels of heaven, while lightning flashed to light their way. The sky opened and the rains poured down. It started with large drops hitting the earth in quick succession. As they hit the parched earth, they sent up large dust balls into the air. For what seemed a long time the village and the fields were covered in a thick cloud of dust. Drought had parched the land for three long years, so that the soil greedily sucked in each drop. The fragrance of the earth rose, pervading the air in all eight directions.

The lovely smell of earth reached Bakkireddy in the cattleshed. He sat up on the cot, inhaling the perfumed air, and filling his lungs. Greedily, avariciously, he breathed in again and again, gathering it all in, like a miser heaping diamonds and pearls in his treasury. The fragrance stirred every cell in his body and kindled a primordial hunger that surged and raged through him. He lifted his head and looked. He saw his bulls chewing the cud; he saw the luxuriant hair on their necks. He saw his plough standing against the wall and its sharp, well-shaped blade. He felt an intense itching in his hands that caused him to open and close them in fists.

The darkness that had engulfed the earth was so thick it felt like a weight on the shoulders. The rain fell in torrents of water as if a thousand elephants were blasting it from their trunks or heaven itself was emptying gigantic tubs all in one great deluge. The rain struck and lashed the earth and everything that stood on it. A howling wind roared out of the northeast thrashing the leaves and branches of the trees; even the great trunks shook in the blasts. Lightning tore open the skies and thunder crashed and rumbled from one end of the horizon to the other. The rain poured across the land in streaks. As the soil grew soggy, the water began to flow in small rivulets that met and joined others to form regular streams that filled up the potholes and puddles of the lowlands which in turn emptied into the river. Already in flood the river surged over its sandy bed, churning up a frothy foam, sweeping in its wake trees, shrubs, and branches. The water was a yellowish brown except for the advancing edge, which frothed a shade of white. The volume of water swelled as it rushed toward the dams of the agricultural tank. Rocked and stupefied by the fierceness of the storm, the villagers huddled in their houses. Men, women, and children wrapped themselves snugly in sheets and slept. Only a few old people remained awake listening to the fury of the storm.

Bakkireddy got up from his cot. He untethered the bulls and brought them out of the cattleshed. Then he took up the plough and yoke and put them on his shoulders. He found his cattle-prod in the eaves of the shed and grasped it firmly. Clucking to the bulls, he brought them out into the street. It was deserted; every door was shut tight against the raging storm. The water spilled down the streets slopping against the walls and plinths of the houses. Making his way by the intermittent lightning flashes, he passed through the streets of the village until he found himself beyond the western boundary, the tamarind groves and aloe hedges behind him, and at the edge of Roadside Land. He lowered the plough and yoke from his shoulders. In a minute, he had the bulls yoked and was hitching up the plough with ropes and thongs. He took his upper cloth off, wrapped it about his head, and rolled up his loin cloth tightly around his waist.

He looked out over the land as it was lit up in the lightning flashes. The five acres were divided up into eight fields of unequal size by dikes. All of the fields were flooded with the water that rushed over the dykes. At the southern edge stood the peepal tree, its branches flailing about and twisting in the brutal wind. Plough handle in his left hand and the cattle-prod in his right, Bakkireddy stepped into the fields with his bulls, much the way a baby crawls on all fours into his mother's lap. He pushed down on the plough handle and prodded the bulls. They lurched forward and the shear of the plough ripped open the earth with a splattering of mud.

The rain continued to fall incessantly. The wind blew harder and harder, constantly shifting direction, whipping the leaves and smaller branches off the trees, blowing them who knows where. Rainwater ran down every part of his body. His turban was soaked and heavy and slipped down on his shoulders; he pulled it off and threw it on the dyke. He was naked save for his loincloth. The cold wind assailed him mercilessly until his body and teeth rattled under the pelting rain that left his skin numb.

He ploughed two of the fields and entered a third. When he hit a new furrow he swayed and fell, but lifted himself again and hobbled along behind his plough. The pain in his hip and spine felt like a spear tip. Soon it was almost beyond him to lift his foot and take a step forward. He panted heavily, the sound rising above the rough hissing of the bulls. Fatigue had all but conquered him. Gradually the pace of the plough slowed. But his grip on the plough handle and driving stick loosened not a bit.

Ploughing

By the first hours of dawn the rain had stopped. The sky was blue and clear with not a wisp of a cloud to be seen anywhere. It looked so innocent and guileless one wondered how it could be the same sky that had wrecked such havoc the previous night. The wind was still and so were the leaves of the trees. Trees that had had their heads bent to the ground much of the night now stood erect, wet, and still. The leaves and branches that had been whipped off lay scattered everywhere half-buried in the sand and mud. And with the first light of dawn, Bakkireddy's wife woke up on her sleeping mattress. She rose and went directly to the cattleshed. She could see the mattress and pillow on the cot. But her husband was nowhere to be seen. She turned and saw that the bulls were not there either. Then she saw that the plough, which had been placed against the wall was not there nor was the yoke or its ropes or thongs. In a glance, she saw that the cattle-prod was missing from its place in the eaves.

Now, she had lived with Bakkireddy for forty years. And it's true, she knew precious little about the world, filled as it was with intrigues and paradoxes. But him, her husband, she knew like the back of her hand. And so, after taking a good look around the cattleshed, she just stood for a long while immobile, as if turned to stone. Then, she let out a terrifying scream. The sleeping neighbours woke up with a start at the sound. And those who were awake and already at work dropped their chores and rushed to the cattleshed. But, she had already left the shed and was on her way moving swiftly down the path to the road. The mud squelched under the soles of her feet and spurted in every direction. Her face was taut, her look grave; she was certain of her destination. Her neighbours caught up with her and trotted along until she stopped at Roadside Land.

By the time the sun had risen, the eight fields were largely under water that lay calm and flat as the wind had dropped. The morning sun was reflected in the mirror-like water. The image of the peepal tree, too, was perfectly reflected in the still waters. In the middle of the third field, the bulls stood ruminating. The plough had fallen to one side. Bakkireddy still held the plough handle in his left hand, the cattle-prod in his right. The body lay in the furrow half-submerged in water. Without so much as gathering up the hem of her sari his wife stepped into the field. The first touch of her foot sent a ripple out over the calm surface of the water that multiplied and fanned out, wrinkling the whole surface.

* * *

A rumour sprang up that quickly reached the village, speeding along every street and by-street and across every threshold. 'Bakkireddy is dead! He lies dead in Roadside Land!' The village churned with the news as people tumbled out of their houses and rushed down the paths that led to Roadside Land. As they ran, the men hoisted up their lower garments and adjusted their upper-cloths; the women tucked in their sari-ends at the waist and gathered up their hair into knots at the back of their heads. The children shot off like arrows from a bow or stones from a sling. The sun was creeping up the sky. The village was still, deserted as if it had fallen to the plague or cholera, but the paths to Roadside Land were all rutted and mired from the feet of the people running along them. They swarmed to the Roadside Land much as the clouds had overshadowed it the day before. They formed a ring, encircling the plough, the bulls, and the dead man, the way a halo forms around the moon in the month of May. The people at the front of the circle turned their heads and passed on the details of what they saw. And the people in the rear stood on tiptoes, craning their necks, to catch a glimpse over the shoulders of the ones in front. They looked, they all looked and saw it for what it was: the left hand holding the plough handle, the right holding the cattle-prod, and the body in the furrow partly submerged. The sight was indelibly imprinted in their minds, just as the image of a man who has struck it on its hood is imprinted in the eyes of a cobra. It was imprinted on their eyes as indelibly as the picture of Dussasana*

---

* Dussasana attempts in full view of the Kuru court, to disrobe Draupadi in order to humiliate her five husbands; Bheema was one of them.

holding Draupadi's hair was stamped on Bheema's eyes. In the years to come, they would blink their eyes millions of times but what they saw today would never be erased. In the years to come they would face and overcome millions of tribulations, but still this scene would probably not be erased from their minds.

The Village

Bakkireddy passed away on the night of Seed Sprout Lunar day.* The Maniam was faithful to his word. He buried Bakkireddy in the Roadside Land underneath the peepal tree as he had asked. Under his personal supervision, every detail of the last rites was carried out meticulously and with great fervour.

The Maniam's ancestors had been chieftains of the province in days gone by. Even to this day, his was the last word, whatever the issue. For example, the State Highway, to the west of the village, was lined on both sides by tamarind trees. Once a year, the tamarind crop came up for auction. Many bidders participated in the

---

* Molakala Pournami – an annual festival, very important for farmers, since it coincides with the arrival of the first rains of the year, the most joyous occasion.

auction. But the last bid was always that of the Maniam. And to the north of the village was the agricultural tank. Once a year, the fish crop was auctioned. Many bidders come to participate in it, too. But the last bid had always been that of the Maniam. The months of May and June were the wedding season. Invitations were sent out to every household in the village, but the first household to receive every invitation had always been the Maniam's. And sometimes it happened that a farmer or an artisan in a far off land lost his livelihood and set out in search of work. Should such a man chance on this village and find work either as a day wager or a sharecropper, the provider of that work had always been the Maniam. And sometimes it happened that a farmer or an artisan of this village, unable to make ends meet, left his hearth and home and migrated to a far off land. And the man who bought up the property of such a man for a throwaway price had always been the Maniam. Now it was merely to keep up this tradition that the Maniam had purchased the Roadside Land, though he, in no way could be said to be lacking in landed property. Therefore, rather than cultivate the land, he let the land lie fallow. The sale document, however, was secure in an iron safe. A padlock as large as your hand hung from its door, for the safe held hundreds of such documents, each attested to by signatures or thumb-impressions, recording thousands of words and numbers. The safe itself sat in a room of its own on the upper floor of his two-story house. And a large padlock hung on the door of that room, too.

So the sale document lay safely in the strongbox with all the others, and the purchased land was left fallow, completely neglected and forgotten. But the man who was buried in the land was anything but forgotten. His memory was alive in the minds of the people. Seated in his office in the Village Council building, the Administrator received many people, who brought him their stories and requests. But never had he had a request like Bakkireddy's. 'After I am gone, brother, it is my wish that my mortal remains be buried in that land under the peepal tree. You must see that this wish of mine is carried out under your own supervision. Give me your word, brother.'

What a strange request!

'You see, brother, when my father was on his death bed, I gave him my word that I would protect the land just as the eyelid protects the eye. The moment my father meets me tomorrow, he will ask, "What have you done with the land, my son?" Then I will answer, looking straight into his eyes, "You can see for yourself, father, I am lying right in the land protecting it the way the eyelid protects the eye. See for yourself."' What a strange conviction! The Administrator wondered whether Bakkireddy would really meet his father and his father would question him that way. At the time he didn't pay much attention to what he took for insane raving. But ever since he saw that left hand holding the plough staff, the right one grasping the cattle-prod, and the body lying half-submerged in the furrow, his opinion had gradually changed.

In the village, it began to be the custom that when the farmers set about harnessing their ploughs to till dry land or wet land they should recall Bakkireddy and his words. 'I am orphaned by my land. Surely you cannot expect me to survive the loss. As things stand, friends, I am left with only two options. I will have to hang myself from a tree or drink pesticide. I will do one of the two. My existence on earth is no longer legitimate, friend. How can I eat, friend? The land was everything to me – I lost it. How can a morsel go down my throat? How can my eyes ever find sleep?'

The villagers seemed to hear these words over the sounds of the plough cutting through the earth and the wind rushing in the leaves and branches. They knew that many and varied were the ways a farmer can die. They had seen or heard of farmers, who unable to stand the loss of their own land had hanged themselves from one of their own trees. They had seen or heard of farmers who could not live down the loss of their land and who walked into their fields in the dead of night to drink pesticide and collapse on the tilled earth. And had they not seen or heard of farmers whose lives had come to an end worn out by an incurable disease? Had they not seen or heard of one cut down by murder or by his own hand? Did they not know of farmers attacked and killed by wild animals or poisoned by venomous snakes? Or, the many who died of starvation or in fatal accidents?

Yes, they had seen or heard of all that and more. But Bakkireddy was the only farmer who had breathed his last ploughing land which had been auctioned off, the only one who overcome by exhaustion had collapsed in the furrow he had been making. They remembered the great tranquillity and serenity of that face looking up from the flooded furrow. And why not? After all it was his own land that he had been lying in, and his own plough handle that his left hand had held, and his own cattle-prod in his right. It was with this knowledge that he breathed his last – tranquil and serene.

Just as they knew that Duryodhana's* obsession with power was as boundless as Yudhishtar's for the truth, they now knew from their own experience that a farmer's

* Duryodhana – the Kuru Prince met his tragic end on account of his boundless and maniacal greed for the realm which justly belonged to Yudhishtira, who in contrast was the epitome of righteousness.

obsession with his land could be equally boundless. This new knowledge made them very thoughtful and melancholy. As they walked towards their own lands to till them, that heavy frame of mind made for twisting and meandering furrows. And when the villagers saw the results of their melancholy, the melancholy gave way to despondency, and then the ploughing meant not only twisting and meandering furrows but an upset in the whole rhythm of their work, which became slow and sluggish. And it was not only the farmers.

As the blacksmith sat by his smithy and kindled the coals and chaff in the forge, unwittingly, his mind would drift to memories of Bakkireddy. 'Friend, you must spare some time for me. My bulls need your service urgently. They need to be shod at once. Can you come to my house with your implements or do you want me to bring the bulls here?' He hears these words through the sounds of the leaping flames in the forge and his hammer ringing on the anvil. And a great gloom descends on him and he wonders whether his smithy forged ploughshares and iron shoes or lethal weapons to annihilate farmers or whether he fed the forge coals and chaff or the bones and flesh of farmers.

So, too, the Karanam gradually ceased to be punctual in reaching his office. It had been his custom to arrive in good time. Not so any longer. These days he came to the office but rarely and when he did, it was at very odd hours. Nor did he any longer open the great wooden case and take out one of the big registers. He had come to believe all manner of sins had taken possession of the shelves and that the registers themselves were swollen with sin. He would have nothing to do with the registers. Instead of sitting at his desk, he sat on the floor with the Gita opened to read verses from it. But he could read no more than four stanzas before the letters on the page began to blur and smudge. He took off his glasses and wiped them with his upper-cloth. But when he began to read again it wasn't the verses of the Gita but the words of the sale document. *The vendor has today delivered to the vendee vacant, physical and peaceful possession and enjoyment of the scheduled property assuring such peaceful possession and enjoyment forever.... In witness whereof the vendor has signed on this Deed of Sale with his own free will and consent on this day, month and year first above mentioned....* And there were three witnesses to the deed and he was one of them. What had he been a witness to? A farmer was orphaned of his land even as Ayodhya* was orphaned by Rama. To that he was a witness. What

* The city of Ayodhya was orphaned when Rama left it on his fourteen-year exile in the forests, and when his father King Dasaratha died, unable to bear the grief of separation.

had he been a witness to? A farmer died of grief from being deprived of his land even as Dasaratha had died of grief from being deprived of his son. To that, he was a witness. He closed the pages of the Gita, put it aside, and leaned back against the wall, staring at the wooden cabinet with stony eyes.

Harischandra

Thus it was that the shack on Temple Street that had been used by the village actors to carry on their rehearsals stood abandoned. All manner of grass and shrubs had grown in front of it. There were stone pyols on either side of the doorway covered in piles of dry leaves as the wind had blown there. The door was locked the day Bakkireddy died and had remained locked ever since. And there were no further rehearsals.

*The path is harsh, alas, O, do walk slowly, girl.**

That was the last verse they had practised. Inside the shack, the musical instruments hung from the walls fuzzed with cobwebs. A few dusty books lay on a bench in the corner; in another, stood a kerosene lamp that

---

* *karuku raal thovalo,bama!*
  mellaganu nadichi raave

had been used during the rehearsals. The kerosene in it had long since evaporated. From the day the rehearsals stopped no actor was ever seen in the vicinity of the shack. The members of the company gradually forgot the verses and dialogues they had so painstakingly memorized for their rehearsals. Only one actor, who was to play the role of King Harischandra, would come slouching along now and then, like a hungry dog looking for food. He would sit on one of the stone pyols, staring at the blackberry bushes that now grew thick before the hut, and recall the sequence they had practised on that last day. The sequence concerned Harischandra and his Queen in exile. They were plodding along a forest path riddled with sharp stones and thorns. The delicate queen who was accustomed to the soft living of the inner palace was sinking under the hardships of the journey. Her feet, split and dripping blood, she drops to the forest floor. The king tries to console her, singing

Harsh is the path, alas, Do walk slowly, O, girl.

When enacting this sequence, the actor spared no effort in trying to express pathos on his face and in his voice but utterly without success. The director made him repeat the verse again and again until his voice grew hoarse. But no matter how hard he tried, he could not bring the required intensity of pathos, either in his expression or in his voice. Today, however, seated on the pyol, the actor inadvertently called mind the left hand holding the plough handle, the right holding the cattle-prod, and the body lying, half-submerged, in the water and, lo, unprompted, tears welled up in his eyes and ran down his cheeks.

The rains had been held back by the heavens for three years. Ant hills grew waist high along the river bed. And the bottom of the agricultural tank was dotted with thorn trees. The villagers started the rehearsals of the play *Sathya Harischandra* in the belief that if the play were staged, it would appease the heavens and would release the rains. But strange are the ways of heaven. For even before the play was staged, the rains arrived in torrents. The agricultural tank filled and overflowed into the sluices. Both the dry land below the mountain and the wet land below the tank were water-logged. The water table had risen and seeped into the wells, filling them to the brim. Water splashed and spluttered in the tanks, in the wells, in the ditches, in pools and ponds. All this had happened in a single day, the Lunar Seed-Sprout day. All that they had given penance for in those three years was requited in a single day. The joy of life that had seeped out of their lives in all that time was given back to them in a single day. But they had not known that on that day they would also have to witness an event that would make them remember a particular event for three generations to come.

The Mute

It was the month of December; it was six months since Bakkireddy's death. During this period the village had changed a great deal. Six months ago the bed of the agricultural tank had lain parched. Today it was filled with water and was beautiful. Six months ago, you needed fifteen fathoms of rope to reach the bottom of a well. Today you could just reach down and pull up a bucket of water. Six months ago, there was nothing to speak of in the dry land under the mountain except pebbles, white-ant hills, cactuses, and patches of slough grass. Today, the very same land was a feast to the eyes, being covered with the bright green leaves, and yellow flowers of the ground-nut crop. The wet land below the agricultural tank six months ago was bleak and infertile, given over to roaming goats and sheep and their herders. The farmers hardly went to their lands and when they did, it was only out of habit. Today the same land buzzed with activity; farmers could be seen toiling on the land from dawn to dusk, and from dusk to dawn the vigilant calling of the guards could be heard.

And the minds of the village people, too, had undergone a great change. They were gradually forgetting the incident they had witnessed on that Seed-Sprout Lunar day. The memory of Bakkireddy's fate rarely crossed their minds and his name cropped up in conversation only sporadically, like the peak of a mountain in a thick fog, like pebbles at the bottom of a murky stream. Slowly, Bakkireddy faded into obscurity. And as the wheel of Time ceaselessly rolled on, his memory might well have been erased from the minds of all in the village. But perhaps that was not to the liking of Time. Perhaps it was the will and design of Time that Bakkireddy's story should, indeed, turn into a legend and be a landmark in the history of the village. Whether it was the fulfilment of that will and design, or just a coincidence, no one really knows, but a strange incident took place toward the end of December. And with that event, the story of Bakkireddy did become a legend in the history of the village, and since the man's story was inseparable from his land, Roadside Land too became a landmark in the geography of the region.

The event had its origins in the Maniam's _doddi_.* The Maniam was singularly proud of his cattle and paid

* Cattleshed.

special attention to their care. He had altogether some thirty head in his herd – cows, bulls, steer, heifers, and calves. The doddi was a spacious one and only a stone's throw away from his two-storied house. Inside the stonewalled enclosure were two tall haystacks and in one of the corners a well with a large drinking trough beside it. A mute boy of fourteen was in charge of the herd. Every day, by the time the sun stood at four fathoms high over the village, the boy would let the cattle out. As they moved along, he walked behind them, his flute stuck into his waistband, a food pouch dangling from his shoulder. The cattle grazed on the fallow lands of the Maniam's property, on the uncultivated lands surrounding the village, on the banks of the river, and slopes of the mountain. The boy knew where to find good grass in the different seasons of the year. As the cattle grazed, the boy would sit in the shade of a large rock or a tree and play his flute. When the sun reached mid-sky, he would open his food pouch and eat what was there, then wash his hands and drink from a pond or stream nearby. At sundown he brought the cattle back into the doddi. He would draw water from the well and fill the trough. When the cattle finished drinking, he would tether each animal to its stake. Then he would take a leisurely bath and go up to the Administrator's house, where he would be served his meal on a banana leaf. From there, he would go up to the village square to meet his friends and chat with them in his sign language. And when the sounds of the village evening died down he would return to the doddi, to a rickety cot provided for him in its corner.

Though the Maniam had utter confidence in the boy's husbandry, he came into the doddi once every week to look to their condition. If he spotted a gadfly or tick on an animal, he ordered it removed at once. If any of them seemed at all unwell, he would instantly send away for the veterinary doctor. And if he noticed a worn-out shoe on any of the bulls, he would have it shod the very next day.

The Song

Thus it happened that one day toward the end of December during the first watch of the night, the Maniam came into the doddi, holding a lantern. The mute boy who had been playing his flute while lying on his cot got up and came to him. The Maniam put down his lamp and asked, 'How are the pregnant ones?'

'They are fine, Ayya,' the boy replied in his sign language 'Three of them will calve very soon. Most certainly in three or four days.'

The Maniam took his lantern and inspected the three cows closely. He saw that they were healthy and that their bellies were large. He nodded in satisfaction and said, 'You said they would calve in three or four days; how can you be so certain, boy?'

'I know, Ayya, because I was the one who took them to Suddapilli to get them mated,' answered the boy.

'Yes, I remember now, that was in the month of April.' The Maniam counted the months on his fingers and said, 'You're right, there. We should see the calves in three or four days, then.'

He put the lantern down again and turned to the mute boy. 'There is something I want you to do now.'

'What is that, Ayya?' the boy asked, then folded his arms across his chest.

'From today on, you will look after only these three cows. Don't do any other work until they have calved.'

'What about the other cattle, Ayya?'

'I will arrange for someone else to look after them. Your only concern will be the welfare of these cows. See to it they are well watered and at the proper times. Take them out to graze only when the day cools and don't take them very far or it will tire them out. Just take them to places not far from the village.'

'Yes, Ayya.'

The Administrator noticed a gadfly on the back of one of the cows, squashed it with a single slap, and wiped the blood against a stone pillar. 'If only they all gave birth to bull calves,' he said with a hopeful enthusiasm, 'by god, I will build a wall of gold.'

'I think they will indeed be bull calves, Ayya,' signed the boy, 'for I have vowed that I will go to Pakala Temple* if these cows give birth to bull calves.'

'Pakala? No, I would rather send you to Tirupathi. There you'd have much more fun. You could have your head tonsured and take a dip in the holy pond and worship the great deity.'

'Yes, Ayya, and then in lower Tirupathi I will buy myself a new flute,' the mute boy grinned in the light of the lantern.

'That's right. Now you should go to sleep.' He picked up the lantern and walked off about four paces before turning and asking, 'And, boy, where will you take the cows to graze tomorrow?'

'You said it should be a nearby place.' And after a minute's thought, he signed, 'What about Roadside Land, Ayya, it's not far off.'

---

* The temple of Murugan at Pakala is less popular than the one on Tirupathi Hills; it is also closer to Ontillu.

'Yes, yes, that's the ideal place. No one has stepped into that land for six months. The grass has grown luxuriously. Yes, take the cows there, and do take good care of them.'

The following day, when the sun had cooled down, the boy led the three pregnant cows to Roadside Land. The five acre plot was roughly rectangular in shape. During the last six months neither a foot nor a hoof had stepped on it, as it belonged to none other than the Maniam himself. For the very same reason, no one had ventured to hay the grass or graze their cattle on it. With no hitch or hindrance, the grass had grown freely and luxuriantly and the land appeared to be a massive green five-acre carpet. The grass was of all varieties, like slate grass with its round succulent blades and sleeping grass with its thin pointed blades and so on and so on.

The three cows dropped their heads and fell to grazing right away. They swished their tails in pleasure, as they tasted the fresh savoury grass. Their neck bells rang continuously as they swung their heads left and right foraging. In the middle of the land, there was an abandoned well in the shade of the light green coin-sized leaves of a thorn tree. Near it grew a beech tree with its larger, palm-sized dark leaves. A flock of sparrows were roosting in the thorn tree, a flock of parrots in the beech tree. The birds were sending up a great clamour as the evening approached. Not far off from the abandoned well stood the peepal tree – tall, stately, and solemn. Beneath the peepal was the burial mound of Bakkireddy. The mound had sunk only a few inches under the impact of the weather during the six months that had passed. Grass had grown over it, covering it almost completely. Every now and then ripened leaves fell from the tree and landed silently on the mound.

The mute boy went over to the tree and sat down under it, leaning his back against the trunk. He crossed one leg over the other, pulled the flute from his waistband, and began to play. His fingers danced rhythmically over the stops. The cows stopped their avid grazing at the first sound of the notes coming from the flute and turned towards the sound. Standing stock still, as if rooted to the ground, long strands of grass still hanging from the corners of their mouths, they stared wide-eyed at the boy and his flute as if they had sighted a friend. They were used to all the songs he would play on his flute, but not this one. He had never played it before. Apprehension shadowed their large, wondering faces as they stared. The sound was like a death knell and the boy appeared a ghoul. But after a while one by one, they dropped their heads again and returned to grazing. The sun was about a fathom high above the horizon. A cold draught has already sprung up, for it was December. The wind caught the sounds and carried them with it through the trees and over the meadows and fields. The song, to be sure, was a dirge, giving voice to the grief of a mother's womb over the loss of its infants.

Today is Friday
And my courtyard gay
I've sprinkled cow-dung water
Adorned the yard with rice flour lines
Next Friday they'll still be there
For I have no toddlers to crawl about.
Today is Friday
And my courtyard gay
Four I had when young and strong,
God took them all, all are gone.
Next Friday the lines will still be there
It tears my guts, twists my heart
Today is Friday
And my courtyard gay
O birds in the trees, birds in heaven
Scratch out those lines for my womb's ease
O birds in the street, birds on the roof
Peck up the flour for my womb's ease
Today is Friday
And my courtyard gay.

Eee roju sukravaram

Inti mundu kalapi challi pindi muggu vesanu

Vache sukravaram varaku ee muggu chedaradu

Ee roju sukra varam

Vayasulo undaga muggurini kannanu

Mugguru poyaru, neny godralini

Ee roju sukravaram

Pogada chettumeeda puchukalara, chilakallara

Muggunu kelikeyyadi, garbha sokam thagginchandi

Eee roju sukravaram

Peratlo kodipunjulara, kodipettalara

Muggunu cheripeyyandi

Na puthra sokam thagginchandi

Ee roju sukravaram

Intimundu kalapichalli pindimuggu vesanu

Vache sukravaram varaku ee muggu chedaradu

Eee roju sukravaram

Now it had happened that two years before, a woman had miscarried in a rich household. Professional mourners* had come along to sing the dirge for the

---

* Professional mourners (*oppari* in Telugu and Tamil, *rudali* in Hindi) are a caste. They weep at funerals and are paid for it in cash or kind. While weeping they sing different kinds of songs depending on age, gender, and the marital status of the deceased.

unborn child. It was the first and only time the mute boy had heard the song. Though he heard it only that once, it so moved him that he grasped and remembered every nuance of its tune. There had been ten professional mourners, who sat in a circle around the stillborn. As they sang the song, wailing and moaning, they frothed at the mouth, undid their bound-up hair and spread their hair on their shoulders, and tore open their blouses to beat their breasts – all the while rolling on the ground. The boy, who had been standing not far from the scene had felt a tremor in his body and soon found himself wailing in grief. That night, he lay on his cot in the doddi in a delirium, possessed by the song, and its tale of the womb's grief. But for the past two years, however, he had never practised or played it again. And for that matter, today, when he sat down under the peepal tree and put the flute to his lips, he had no intention of playing the song. The flute seemed to play the song of its own accord, nay, an unseen hand seemed to play it. The pathetic scene of two years ago rose up before his eyes. He saw again the circle of professional mourners around the dead foetus, saw again the unbound hair spread over shoulders, and saw again the blouses torn open and the beating of breasts. The tears streamed down the wailing, lamenting faces even as they sang, rolling on the ground in contortions of grief. He saw again the dust cloud that rose over their kicking and writhing bodies. He saw the grief of the womb as if it were a physical object.

The clamour of the sparrows and parrots had long since ceased. The birds were still, stunned into silence by the pathos of the music. And a shiver ran through the boy's body much as it had two years before when he had heard the tune for the first time and beheld the mourners. By and by, he lost the strength to play his flute and his fingers faltered on the stops. Then the flute fell silent and in the eerie quiet, the mute boy sat rigidly still like a statue carved out of rock. The flute dropped into his lap. As he sat there motionless and silent, he heard the neck bells of the cows clanging as if calling for his attention. He turned his head and saw the three of them lying on the grass not far from the mound of earth under the peepal tree. When he noticed what lay in front of each of them, he sprang to his feet as if catapulted. The flute was flung high up into the air. It somersaulted down, falling on the mound. In a leap the boy was beside the cows. A dead calf lay in front of each one and they were licking off the placentas. The boy knelt down and gin-gerly touched the three lumps of flesh. Then, panic-stricken he jumped up and began to sprint towards the village.

The Cows

The level rays of the setting sun fell on the two-storied house of the Maniam. The house was surrounded by a high compound wall with a massive iron gate. The black horse stood outside the iron gate. A groom who had saddled and bridled the horse stood by stroking its mane, as he looked back toward the iron gate. Presently the Maniam emerged from the house, adjusted the upper-cloth across his shoulder. He gave a few instructions to his wife who accompanied him to the threshold to see him off. He pushed open the gate, took the reins from the groom, and placed a foot in the stirrup. Just at that moment he heard what seemed like someone calling and shouting from the western direction, but there were no words to understand in the sound. Then he quickly realized it was the mute boy coming at a run, hooting and waving his arms wildly like a drowning man. The Maniam, his foot still in the stirrup, waited as the boy drew nearer. He came up panting, nearly collapsing, and shouted in his sign language, 'Dead calves! The cows gave birth – to dead calves! Ayya!'

The Maniam tore his foot from the stirrup and in the same motion slapped the boy so hard across the face he fell sideways on the ground. 'Scoundrel! I warned you to take good care of those animals. No doubt you took them to some far-off place, walked them over hill and field, and exhausted them.' The boy scrambled to his feet desperately gesturing, 'No, Ayya, no! I took them nowhere but to Roadside Land. It was there that they gave birth to those calves.'

The Maniam again stepped into the stirrup and mounted, digging his heels into the horse's flanks. The horse galloped off, kicking up clouds of dust. He pulled up at Roadside Land. The three cows still lay on the grass. A small crowd had gathered around the cows and the dead calves, discussing the strange phenomenon among themselves. The Maniam immediately sent for the veterinarian from the village, who rushed to the spot. He gave the cows a thorough examination according to his own long experience and considerable knowledge. Then he washed his hands in the stream, and dried them on his upper cloth. The Administrator eagerly awaited his conclusions. 'According to my reckoning, brother, their wombs were damaged.' 'But how could that happen?' protested the Maniam, 'the last time they calved, they each produced a bull calf perfect as a pearl. This is their second calving, why did it turn out this way now?'

The veterinary put his upper-cloth up on his shoulder and beckoned to the Administrator to come away from the crowd. They walked a little distance off to the abandoned well and sat down on its edge. The Administrator's face was a map of questions. But in giving his considered diagnosis, the veterinarian spoke with caution. 'As you know all too well, brother, I have been veterinarian here for over fifty years, and the science and art was handed down to me by my ancestors, but I've never seen or heard of so strange a thing as this. Three cows aborting at the same time? How is that? True, all three have spoiled wombs, but how did that come about? I thought about the possibilities. Were they grazing on some poisonous weeds or grasses? But I must rule that out because I am completely familiar with the flora and fauna of this province and we have no such poisonous plants or bushes here. Could it be that they had been bitten by some poisonous reptile or snake? But it is illogical that all three should have been stricken at the same time. From all this I deduce ... I deduce ... that.'

'That they were poisoned by someone?'

'Precisely. That precisely is what I think.'

'But who would do that?'

'Indeed. That is the question before us now.'

The Resolve

Seated in a large chair in the upper floor of his two-storied house, the Maniam stared out of the window at a far off range of hills. His face was grim as he considered the dark question that faced him. Who had poisoned his cows? Every cell in his body wrestled with the question. There was no easy answer. Apart from the herd of cattle, he also had a flock of sheep, and another of goats. He owned and cultivated groves of mango, of tamarind, and coconut trees. As for land, he had long since lost count of the number of acres he owned. Yet, the matter of the death of three calves tormented him.

With good reason.

It happened that ten years back, he had had a pet dog that kept him company day and night. When he went out in the mornings to supervise the work in his groves and fields the dog was always at his heel. When he set out to visit neighbouring villages, either on foot or on horseback, the dog would trot along behind him. When he was in his office in the Panchayath Office seeing to his official work, the dog would lie curled up beneath his chair. At night when the Maniam slept the dog would lie close by his couch ready to spring up at the first sound of anything moving. Then one morning, the dog was found lying flat on its back, its legs kicking the air, and its whole body shuddering. The veterinarian was quickly called in and he did all that he could, but could not save the dog. It was his opinion that it had been poisoned. For his part, fond though he was of the dog, the Maniam took the matter lightly enough and was not overly concerned with discovering just what it was that caused its death. But soon enough, he was to pay for his complacency. A fortnight after the dog died, a ghastly incident occurred. In the middle of the night, while he was fast asleep, a masked man had tried to kill him. His first blow missed its target, but the knife chipped a large piece out of the wooden frame of the couch. The Maniam started up and saw the man standing over him, ready to strike a second blow. He grabbed the blade of the knife with his right hand and tried to pull the mask off with his other. The razor sharp edge gashed his fingers and palm, the blood spurting from the wound had sprayed on his face and blinded him. Never releasing his grip on the knife, he struggled with the assailant and managed to pull off the mask, but he could not get a good look at the man because of the blood in his eyes and the man escaped. The Maniam had nearly severed two fingers of his hand in grasping the knife blade so hard that they had to be amputated. It took two months for the stumps to heal and the right hand was permanently maimed. All efforts to uncover the identity of the attacker came to nothing and it remained to this day a mystery. But the Maniam was forced to realize that the poisoning of his dog was a foreshadowing of the event and again and again he berated himself for his complacency.

And now, ten years later, his cows had been poisoned! What could this foreshadow? He got up from the chair and paced the room, for a long time. Then he stood a long time at the window and looked across the village, as if it slumbered peacefully in the moonlight. But for him the moonlight seemed like blood and fire pouring down on the earth. He raised his maimed hand and held it up in the moon rays that poured in the window and saw in a vivid flash the blood spraying from the gashes in his hand. Then he made a pledge, 'I shall not rest until I have caught whoever it was that poisoned my cows. I shall know no rest until I get that done right.'

The Covenant

The next day the Maniam handed over all household responsibilities to his son and all Panchayath affairs to the Karanam. He wanted to be completely free to spend all his time in pursuing his investigation. Who was the criminal who had poisoned his cows? Why? What was the motive? What could it possibly presage? Until he had the answers to these questions he resolved not to pay any attention to other matters, be they domestic or official. So he sent for all his relatives, friends, and well-wishers in his village and the ones in the Province and held conferences with them, seeking their opinions and advice.

Some suggested that all the possible suspects be brought into the doddi and thrashed mightily and that would bring out the truth. Someone said a complaint should be made to the police. Someone else suggested that the goddess Gangamma be propitiated and she would possess the priest and through him would make known the truth. Someone recalled a saint who lived in the Talakona Caves, whose thumb nail, when smeared with a certain ointment, would turn into a magic mirror that would reveal anything anyone was concealing. Someone remembered a gypsy soothsayer who lived in the Kallur Forest and who with her magic rod would unravel any mystery you wished her to. Someone thought of the priest of Parthasarathi Koil of Chennapatnam who was an adept in every branch of science and could put to rest any dilemma you took to him.

The Maniam listened patiently and earnestly to all these opinions and suggestions and diligently set about implementing them.

Thus, the suspects in the village and from the outlying areas were rounded up and brought into the doddi which echoed with their shrieks. Dozens and dozens of bamboo rods were rendered to shreds in the beatings. Complaint after complaint went to the police station. The Goddess Gangamma was propitiated with special rituals. The horse-cart plied ceaselessly between

Ontillu and the Talakona Caves, between Ontillu and Kallur Forest, between Ontillu and Chennapatnam.

And the suspects who were thrashed blurted out many a truth. The police provided many a clue. The goddess Gangamma possessed the priest and through him made many a prophecy. The saint of the Talakona Caves made many a speculation. The gypsy soothsayer of Kallur Forest came out with many hearsay. The priest of Parthasarathi Koil of Chennapatnam suggested many a possibility.

And when these truths, clues, prophecies, speculations, and possibilities were all put together, a yarn was spun. But it was incoherent, incongruous, incomplete, and was in no way to the satisfaction of the Maniam. So he plunged on vehemently redoubling his efforts, for great and unshakeable was his resolve to have the truth.

Winter came and went; spring passed; and summer arrived. The iron tyres of the horse cart had worn out and were replaced. The horse's hooves had to be re-shod at least four times. During all these months, the Maniam was hardly ever at home. Most of the time he was travelling about on his quest. He had aged noticeably; his face was creased with wrinkles and his walk was a kind of limp, bent over like an old man. Nevertheless, the all-consuming questions in his heart burned ceaselessly, refusing to be quenched. By the end of the month of May, many, many more truths, clues, prophecies and speculations, hearsays, and possibilities had been gathered. And when they were sifted, analysed, conjectured with, and pondered over, delved into and pieced together, lo, a myth was born. And the myth went like this:

The rains poured down as if all the clouds of heaven had melted into one great flood. The wind blew hard enough to think it might uproot the mountains. Earth and sky shook in the thunderous rumbling and the sky was rent by the flashing bolts of lightning. Undeterred by the fury of the storm, a plough was moving in Roadside Land, a sixty-year-old man was plodding behind it, his left hand was holding the gripping of the plough handle and his right the cattle-prod. Save for his loincloth, he was naked. The cold wind assailed him mercilessly. His body shook and his teeth chattered, chilled to the bone. The stinging rain pierced his numb skin like the points of spears.

He had already covered two fields and had entered the third. Under the onslaught of wind and rain, he swayed then fell, but got up and hobbled on behind the plough. His spine and all the joints of his body racked with pain. Gradually the pace of the plough slowed, he could no longer take another step; fatigue had finally conquered him.

The sound of his heavy breathing could be heard above the hissing noise of the plough and the panting of the bulls. But the grip of his left hand on the plough handle and his right on his cattle-prod did not slacken. He pulled up the bulls and stopped, the ropes went limp. He was panting harshly and his legs buckled under him. He sank to his knees behind the plough. The storm never let up in its fury. He knew his time was up. He raised his exhausted head to look at the five acres of his Roadside Land one last time. Tears brimmed in his eyes and ran down his cheeks mixing with the streaming rain. Then the Five Elements came forth and took him into their embrace and spoke to him and said: 'O righteous man, grieve not. You gave your word to your father that you would keep and protect the land as eyelid protects the eye. Do not think you have broken your word or have failed your father. We stand witness to the fact that every clod and particle of this land has been soaked and drenched by your sweat. In this very land, your blood, flesh, and bones were consumed. And in this land, your childhood and youth and all the stages of your life were used up and extinguished.

'Inexorably you slogged on for so many years and got little more reward than ambali* for your stomach and a loin cloth to cover yourself. And even that little that you

---

* A gruel of coarse rice.

had was not the motive for your toil. In truth, you toiled out of sense of your duty as a farmer and for the love of your land. We stand witness to that. And in so far you have toiled tirelessly, compelled by so noble an idea, you have assuredly risen in our eyes to be a Karmayogi. This land, O Karmayogi, furrowed for so many years by your plough alone, shall not be turned by another man's plough; this land cultivated by you till now shall not be cultivated by anyone else. We are making a covenant to this effect. Lo! From this day onwards anyone who eats the produce of this land shall see their breasts shrivel. They shall have abortions. And they shall go barren. From this day onwards, any animal that grazes this land will see its udders shrivel. They shall have abortions. And they will go barren. O Karmayogi! The covenant made on this day shall remain in force as long as the sun and the moon traverse the heavens. O, Karmayogi! We, the Five Elements, welcome you and merge you with us.' Where upon the old man fell sideways into the flooded furrow and lay half-submerged in the water.

This then was what the Maniam's six-month-long inquest finally arrived at. And this was the answer that was finally concluded to satisfy the tormented questioning of the Maniam and his relatives and friends and well-wishers.

How did this myth come into being? Who began it? Who worked it up into its final form? No one knows. What was its origin? How many stages did it pass through before it reached its final shape? No one knows. All we can say is that the lifeless egg transforms itself into a sentient one, and from the sentient egg a hideous larva emerges and the larva turns into a motionless pupa and from the pupa emerges a butterfly of gorgeous colours. Isn't this the pattern of myth making? Even so, milk that is liquid when drawn from the milch cow mysteriously turns into semi-solid curds, and the curds when churned turn to butter and the butter when clarified turns into fragrant ghee. Isn't this the way that myths are shaped? It doesn't matter how the myth began or who started it or who gives it its final shape. It's not a matter of where or how it had its beginnings, or how many stages it has gone through; the end is that this myth found a home in the hearts of the people of the village and in the heart of the Maniam.

And so he called off his investigation and ended his quest. One day he led a large number of labourers to Roadside Land. They carried crowbars and spades on their shoulders. Under his instructions, they dug a knee-deep trench around the whole of the five acres that made up Roadside Land. Then hundreds of stone slabs, each one of them three fathoms high, that had been carted down from the quarry, were set up side by side perpendicularly with almost no space between them, sealing the land from any possible intrusion by man or animal.

Now, it belonged only to the soul of Bakkireddy. The Maniam heaved a sigh of relief and became his usual self again; ready to resume his domestic and official duties.

The Thicket

Three decades passed. Seed-Sprout Lunar day came and went thirty times. All the while, Roadside Land increased in trees and became a thicket of woods that was known as Bakkireddy Thicket. During that time, no human foot nor any animal hoof stepped on the land. The wall was never penetrated. No knife, no axe ever struck a branch of a single tree. They grew without hindrance and of all kinds in great abundance – thorn trees, flame trees, fig trees, peepal trees, banyan trees – each one competing with the other in height, girth, and foliage. Thick broad-leaved creepers entwined the trees from trunk to the highest branches and formed a canopy so thick that not the smallest ray of sunlight or moonlight ever reached the ground.

If one stood at the outskirts of the village and looked all around, he would find, as far as he could see, fields of paddy, sugar cane, millet, and ground nut. And topping them all would loom Bakkireddy Thicket like a giant among dwarfs.

And so, it stands even today.

Epilogue

We who live in Ontillu village believe that long, long ago, a fierce battle took place between Rama and Ravana; Lachmana was swooned in the battle and that Hanuman had flown off to Sanjeevi Mountain to bring it back the special curing herbs that grew on it. On his return wearied by the huge burden that he carried as he flew, he swooped down and rested his big toe for a fraction of a second on the big rock to the south of the village to catch his breath. The moment he touched it, that rock was sanctified. And became known in due time as Hanuman Rock. No one had to teach us this legend; we took it in with our mother's milk. Of course there are people who doubt and question the credibility of such events, but there are as many who consider it a divine occurrence and earnestly and reverentially believe it to be true. But, no matter, whether believer or non-believer, the rock has become a permanent landmark in the history and geography of the village. And we worship there every day and celebrate Hanuman Festival each year in the month of April.

* * *

We of Ontillu village believe that about two generations ago, a chieftain who governed this province ordered the construction of an agricultural tank to be built to the north of the village, but the embankment that was constructed caved in each time the tank was filled right at its midpoint again and again. And that the Goddess Gangamma proclaimed that the breach would be sealed if a maiden was to be buried at the exact point of the break and that the chieftain's youngest daughter, Chinamma came forward and offered herself for the sacrifice and was buried in the breach. Ever since, the embankment has remained solid and never failed again. We learned this legend from our fathers and grandfathers. Of course, there are people who doubt the truth of this legend, but there are as many who hold it true and believe it was a divine event. No matter, believed or not, Chinamma Temple has become a landmark in the history and geography of the village. Every Friday we offer worship to Chinamma and celebrate her Festival every year in August.

* * *

We who live in Ontillu village believe that long, long ago, about three decades ago, there lived in our village a sixty-year-old farmer by the name of Bakkireddy and that he lived an honest and righteous life cultivating his five acres of land and that the land had to be sold off in auction to pay the debts he incurred trying to save it from drought and that on a rainy night he died from sheer fatigue while tilling the fields that were no longer his and that the Five Elements made a covenant with him that the land would never be cultivated by anyone else ever and that over the years a thicket of trees had grown up in the land and had become known as Bakkireddy Thicket. Some of us learned this legend from our fathers and mothers. Some of us witnessed it ourselves when we were children and remember it still. Of course, there are people who doubt the truth of the story, but there are quite as many who think it was a divine occurrence and stand reverently by it as truth. But, whether one is a believer or not, the Bakkireddy Thicket is a landmark in the history and geography of the village. And anyone entering the village from the west would always find himself taking off his turban and dipping his head as he passes Bakkireddy Thicket.

About the Author and the Translator

Author and Translator

KESAVA REDDY was born into a family of farmers in Chittoore district, Andhra Pradesh. After his early education, he obtained his MBBS degree from Pondicherry Medical College and did a Postgraduate Diploma in Dermatology from CMC, Vellore and began working at CSI Hospital. He is a well-known novelist and has written dozens of short stories and many novellas. In his writings he addresses many of the important social problems in India like poverty, prejudice, and superstition, and encourages people to be socially responsible. He successfully bridges the idealistic and the popular styles of literature. He runs a clinic in Nizamabad town.